Divine

Appointments

CYNTHIA NAULT SMITH

Divine

Appointments

By

Cynthia Nault Smith

DEDICATION

To the men in my life: Dennis, Greg, Grant, and Xavier.

"A drop of ink may make a million think"
Lord Byron

CYNTHIA NAULT SMITH

CONTENTS

CYNTHIA NAULT SMITH

FOREWORD

On a cold and snowy December day in a hospital in Appleton, Wisconsin, a tiny little child entered this world. This child fought its way into this world and fought its way through this world.

The child's mother had some complications during birth, making her unable to push and assist the baby. Labor had been long and slow. With no signs of progress at hand, the doctor gave in to his fatigue and went home. This, of course, made nature decide to move things along a little faster.

With the mother unable to push, and the doctor on his way home, this was when the baby decided to be born. Strong and stubborn, the little one fought a tough fight. The only person who was there in the mother's room was an equally stubborn Catholic nun.

The determined nun prayed, encouraged the mother, and helped any way she could. This holy woman was thus the first to hold the little girl as she made her debut. She lovingly handed the child to the mother, saying, "I don't know what this little girl is supposed to do in life, but God surely has a reason why she was born."

That little girl was me.

I would love to tell you that I led a charmed life and God's reason for me being here became clear almost immediately as I grew up. But that would not be true. I have spent the better part of my life trying to figure out what God's reason was. I was told the story of my birth many times, and every time the story included the faithful nun's declaration.

Every time I heard it, I wondered about my purpose in life. It's not a bad thing to think about. I sure hoped she was right. It was reassuring to feel that God had a special reason for me to exist.

Back then, I was looking ahead, and the future, like it always is, was cloudy. From where I stand now, I can tell you about my marriage, my kids, my grandkids, and I can see how God pointed my life in those directions. Of course, I am still not sure what my ultimate purpose in life is.

As I look back at my life, I visualize my experience as a series of doors. The doors are different colors, shapes and sizes, which represent the size and intensity of the decisions I made along the way. At every stage of my life, there was a door to the right and a door to the left. The left door always led to the hardest possible path. That was the door I chose most of the time. My stubborn nature helped me into this world, but it wasn't always my friend. Time after time, I chose the door that led to pain, heartache, and ultimately a dead end.

All through my life, a few things were consistent. The two most important things were always my family and my faith. My parents never gave up on me. They loved me through (and despite) every wrong decision I ever made.

I had always had issues with the Catholic religion, but I never questioned my faith. I loved God deeply as I grew up, and I consistently spent much time pondering Him, His actions and His motives.

In my early twenties, I was stumbling through life. I was a bird with a broken wing and no nest. As I stood in the hallway of my life, trying to decide which dead-end door to open next, there came a knock on a third door that was loud and clear. I was intrigued. I cracked open the door of my heart. There stood the Lord. His arms were wide open, and he welcomed this wounded soul into His loving arms of grace.

God helped me feel safe in His arms. Comforted, I became curious, and then I began to open new doors. This time with the Lord at my side, the new doors I opened led to some beautiful and unexpected blessings. In faith, I stepped onto the path of marriage and parenthood. In faith, I began to embark on a long and winding walk with God. These are paths I still walk today.

My life of faith has been a rag to riches story. At the time I gave my life to Christ, I had seldom opened a Bible. But with God's guidance, I began to study His Word.

As I became seasoned in the scriptures, I was asked to help with some classes, and eventually I was asked to lead and teach other women. I led quite a few of my own Bible Studies. Eventually, I began to see that my service to God in this way might have been part of what the nun told my mother all those years ago.

My life began to grow and flower. My path had become a path of service to the Lord. I was blessed to serve on a mission team that took the Gospel to India. Our mission team taught pastors and church planters there how to bring the gospel into the villages of India through story boards. On my first trip to India, I finally understood. My mission was to share the Gospel of Jesus Christ wherever God wanted me to. My job was to spread the Good News of God's love with this world in any way I could.

That mystery was solved. But new questions arose. My poor brain is always full of questions, mysteries, thoughts, and what-if's. I suspect it will always be like that.

A couple of years ago I started writing a Christian blog. I wanted to work on my writing skills so I could continue to spread the Word of God. My blog has been a combination of head knowledge and heart knowledge liberally doused with personal life observations, and flavored with a dash of speculation and a heaping tablespoon of wonder. You hold in your hand the distilled spirits of that semi literary adventure.

I love writing! I'm working on the next book now, and if it is God's will, it will be done before long.

My purpose in writing these pages is to give people (like you) a sense of hope and help them find their way to a new life in Jesus. For long standing Christ followers, I hope to offer some of the insights that I have had over the years.

I am no theologian. I offer no footnotes, nor do I consider this a work of reference or a textbook. I have presented my thoughts in a series of short chapters. If I have done my job well, I hope that as you read this book, you may find yourself smiling, nodding your head and every now and then letting out a laugh. I am sure there will be a few eye-rolls along the way.

I pray that you find hope in these pages. I pray this work will help you take a closer look at the role of God in your life. Perhaps something I have written will give you a chance to try out some new and different ideas about the life of a Christian in today's messy and noisy world.

My prayer is that you too will open that door on your journey through life that brings you into the arms of our Loving Lord and Savior Jesus Christ.

A simple note about Bible verses as they appear in this book. The New International Version is the default book used throughout the text. When there is no mark, think NLV. Translations other than the New International Version are marked, NLT for the New Living Translation, and ESV for the English Standard Version.

1.

JOSEPH

"Y ou meant evil against me, but God meant it for good."

If we look back on our lives, we can probably find someone to whom we could have said those very words. It happened to Joseph, just as it happened to many others in the Bible. The story of Joseph is in the book of Genesis. I love Joseph! He started off as a young man who was quite full of himself. He was his father's favorite out of twelve sons. Favoritism is an important factor in this story.

Joseph was Jacob's favorite son because he was born to Rachel. Rachel, you may recall, was the love of Jacob's life. Jacob had other wives and concubines, but Rachel was top of the list in his heart. Joseph was the golden child. Because he was the favorite child, his eleven brothers were jealous of him. Sibling rivalry can cause many family problems. In Joseph's case, it almost led to his death by fratricide.

Joseph's brothers were so jealous of him they tried to kill him. They tossed Joseph into a dried up well and left him there to die. Before they could leave the scene of the crime, however, a caravan of merchants came on the scene. They hauled him up out of the well and sold him as a slave to the merchants, who were on their way to Egypt.

The brothers left the scene believing that they had gotten rid of Joseph for good. They killed a goat and covered Joseph's garment with some of the goat's blood. When they went home for the night, they took the bloody coat with them.

They took the ornate robe back to their father and said, "We found this. Examine it to see whether it is your son's robe." He recognized it and said, "It is my son's robe! Some ferocious animal has devoured him. Joseph has surely been torn to pieces." (Genesis 37:32-35)

Jacob's life was shattered. He tore his clothes and put on sackcloth. He mourned for many days. He was inconsolable. Joseph was eventually sold to one of the Pharaoh's officials. Joseph spent many years in captivity and in and out of prison. His faith in God never wavered and his attitude remained positive. He remained obedient to God and as a result, he won favor with God in all he did.

Joseph had a talent for administration, and he rose to be second in command in Egypt. His brothers had to humble themselves to him to save their lives from starvation because of a famine. Joseph forgave them. He welcomed them back into his life. He fed and sheltered them, their livestock, and all of those they loved.

Joseph is often referred to as a foreshadowing of Christ. They both had enemies that wanted them dead. They both found favor with God. They both were rejected by others. They both had tender, forgiving hearts. Both were wise and strong, and they were saviors to their people. Both were able to say, "You meant evil against me, but God meant it for good."

And here is the good news for us. We can all relate to someone meaning to do us evil. But God can always turn it all to the good if we remain faithful. Isn't it wonderful to know that we are in such good company?

As children of God, we are in God's favor. He will always protect us. He will turn the worst into the best for us. We are His beloved children and we were created to work for His glory. There is no evil so powerful that God cannot turn it around and make it work out for our best. We just need to remain faithful and obedient. No matter what was thrown at Joseph, he just kept going. Jesus experienced the worst in every way, but he remained faithful and obedient to the Father.

So, we are also encouraged to remain faithful and obedient, no matter what this world throws at us. We are His beloved children. However, God doesn't have favorites. He loves our stained and tattered souls more than words can say. He sent His son to bear our sins so that we won't get crushed by them. We can be free to enjoy God, life and the beauty all around us, each and every day.

So live, love and enjoy. Live in gratitude that you don't have to carry that garbage bag full of your sins around every day. Each day is a new day to glorify God with praise. Empty the garbage in your life and use the bag to collect the blessings!

"You meant evil against me, but God meant it for good."

2.

THE COAT OF MANY COLORS

One fascinating thing about the Bible is the way threads of meaning are woven together all through the book from Genesis to Revelation. God used many literary techniques to tell the whole story. Over and over we see ideas in the Old Testament that continue to develop and are then brought to fulfillment in the New Testament.

God's creativity as an author was limitless. He used dreams, prophets, visions, and poetic expression to engage our imaginations. There are miracles, proverbs, parables, adventure stories, poetry, songs, and even love letters.

Old Testament stories and prophecies are seen in new ways in the New Testament. Themes are repeated, events are tied together, and new ideas are built on the foundation of older ones.

The Bible is connected, chapter after chapter, book after book. There is not a word that is not meant to be there and there is a reason for every word, every sentence and every paragraph. The books of the Bible are glorious threads that are woven together in a master tapestry.

Studying the Bible is much like peeling away the layers of an onion. The more we work at it, the more layers are revealed. In the process we can see how the different parts are connected. We can see how the Old Testament sets the stage for the New Testament.

This is not a coincidence. This is exactly what we would expect from the living word of a living God.

One literary device God uses in the Bible is foreshadowing. We see this in the story of Joseph. In the last chapter I talked about Joseph's life as a kind of preview of the life of Jesus. Through foreshadowing, God shows us how different layers of divine truth are connected.

Another often used device is symbolism. Because God used symbols constantly in the Bible, we would be wise to take a closer look at the story of Joseph and his famous coat. We should expect that such a unique garment would have special significance.

The story of the coat of many colors is a favorite of both children and adults. There have been songs and plays written about it. It must have been quite magnificent. Its beauty caused Joseph's brothers to be jealous. It may have been the thing that pushed Joseph's brothers to contemplate his murder.

I have thought about that coat many times. What is the purpose of a coat? A coat covers and protects one from the elements. In Joseph's case it was a sign of the deep love and special relationship that existed between himself and his father. It was also a sign of the love and protection God would provide during Joseph's time in Egypt.

During that time there was a great famine. The ruler of Egypt put Joseph in charge of the nation's grain supplies. It was his job to ration and distribute these food stores to stave off starvation for the people of Egypt and the surrounding lands. The famine led Joseph's brothers to go to Egypt in hopes of buying the grain their family and their servants needed to survive. In the course of events that followed, Joseph and his brothers were reconciled.

It's easy to see parallels with the story of Jesus as we look at these ideas. Jesus had the love and protection of God the

Father. When we have faith in Christ we are under the cloak of His love and protection. We enjoy a special relationship with Him. Our sins are covered by His death and resurrection. God's love shelters us from the storms of this life. We are protected from the ravages of sin. We are reconciled to God through the saving grace of Christ.

Joseph's beautiful garment must have been very expensive. We can assume it cost his father a great deal to have it made. Likewise, a great price was paid to buy our salvation from sin and death. It cost Jesus His life. It cost God the human life of his only Son.

What about the different colors that made Joseph's coat so special? I believe the different colors represent the different races of man that Jesus came to save. His message was for the people of every race, every tribe and every nation. The grace of God is for all mankind.

After this I saw a vast crowd, too great to count, from every nation and tribe and people and language, standing in front of the throne and before the Lamb. (Revelation 7:9 NLT)

Joseph's coat must have reminded people of a rainbow. We all know the story in Genesis of Noah and the Ark. When the flood was over, God placed a rainbow in the sky as a covenant that he would never again destroy the earth by a flood. Much later, in Revelation, a different rainbow is mentioned.

The one sitting on the throne was as brilliant as gemstones – like jasper and carnelian. And the glow of an emerald circled his throne like a rainbow. (Revelation 4:3 NLT)

Both of these rainbows remind us that God loves all the different people who make up this earth. He hung the rainbow in the sky in Genesis and he placed a rainbow around the throne of Christ in Revelation. God's love covers and protects His people all the way through the Bible, in the present day and through eternity.

God carefully structured the various parts of the Bible so they would work together from beginning to end. God's love and faithfulness weaves the days of our lives together from beginning to end. He is a master craftsman. He has a plan of His own design that will take the threads of our individual lives and work them together into a single tapestry. There is a place in His design for each of us.

The finished product will be a great masterpiece. It will hang above His throne at the very center of Heaven. It will be the greatest work of art anyone has ever seen. It will be visible from every part of Heaven. This will be Creation's final rainbow. It will be the most amazing and beautiful thing ever created. What glory that will be!

May all of us find hope and joy in the beauty that God has created in our lives. May the hands of our Heavenly Father weave our souls together into a work of indescribable beauty. May we realize that we are all part of the kingdom of our loving God. May he reign forever!

3.

WRONGFULLY IMPRISONED

If you had been wrongly imprisoned for many years and suddenly, without warning, someone handed you the keys to unlock the prison doors and escape to freedom, what would you do? Would you grab the keys and run? Or would you be suspicious of a trap, and decline the opportunity to be free?

So many of us are in prison and are unaware of it. We are in prisons of our own making. We have placed walls and bars around ourselves spiritually, physically, mentally or emotionally. Perhaps we have been held back, overlooked or neglected. Maybe we have been lied to by ourselves or by someone else. It may be that the lie has simmered inside of us for years. Then one day we notice the bars we have put up around us and realize we are being held captive. We can live behind these bars for years before we realize the truth and try to break free.

Words have great power. They can be more dangerous than physical weapons. Bodily injuries can heal. The pain caused by mental and emotional wounds can last a lifetime. When we were young, we were very impressionable. We didn't understand the power of harsh words. Sometimes when we were assaulted in this way, we believed we deserved it.

Physical and sexual abuse is reprehensible. So is verbal and emotional abuse. Criminal assailants are put behind bars. With verbal and emotional abuse, it's usually the victims that are in prison for years. People who are labeled dumb, fat, stupid, ugly, slow, or inferior feel the effects for years. When a person is made to feel "less than" it puts them in an emotional prison. The more the abuse is repeated, the longer and darker the sentence becomes. It can even become a death sentence.

The Apostle Paul spent a great deal of his life in a real prison. After he became a believer, he was repeatedly beaten and jailed. But his faith did not waver. He was willing to die for his faith if need be. He believed that words mattered, especially the words of the Gospel. He believed with all his heart that Jesus had come to be the Word of God in human form.

In the beginning, the Word already existed. The Word was with God, and the Word was God. He existed in the beginning with God. God created everything through him, and nothing was created except through him. The Word gave life to everything that was created, and his life brought light to everyone. The light shines in the darkness and the darkness can never extinguish it. (John 1: 1-5 NLT)

I recently read "The Heavenly Man," the autobiography of Liu Zhenying. This man was a modern day version of the Apostle Paul. He became known as Brother Yun. Because of his great faith, the Gospel spread throughout much of China. But he paid a great price.

Brother Yun was imprisoned for years in China because of his faith. He was often badly beaten, just as Paul had been. It did not stop him from preaching the Gospel. He was willing to die for his faith if need be. Like Paul, he was willing to suffer and be imprisoned for as long as there was breath in his body. Both men worked from their prison cells in an effort to continue to share their faith.

One day, after many years in prison, Brother Yun walked out of the front doors of the prison. He wasn't released by the authorities. He literally walked out of the open prison doors, strolled down the street, hailed a taxi and went home. No one knows how or why, but all the prison doors between his cell and the outside world had been left open. The prison guards made no move to stop him. Instead, they acted as if they were completely unaware of him. He walked right past them to freedom. He is still the only person who has ever escaped from the notorious Zhengzhou Maximum Security prison.

Whatever prison you are living in, the keys to your jail cell are within your reach. If you don't see that, you have been listening to the deceiver, the father of lies. He is the one who wants to steal your happiness, your hope and your joy.

Christ wants to give your freedom back to you. He wants to hand you the keys to your prison. He wants you to walk beside him into freedom and into the safety of His embrace forever. He wants you to know that you are loved beyond measure. He gave his life so that you don't have to listen to the lies. He is waiting to tell you how beautiful and capable you are. He wants you to know that you are loved, and that there is a path for you that only you can walk.

You were created to be an incredible person. Your unique personality was known to God before the earth was ever formed. That is how loved you are. You are so important that Jesus himself came to earth to die in your place. He bought you with His blood. Your ransom has been paid. Now you have the right to a place with Him for all of eternity. All you have to do to claim your spot is to turn your life over to Him.

So grab those keys! Unlock the gates of whatever hell you are living in. You have the power to walk right out of the front door of your prison just like Brother Yun did. Cast off the lies and embrace the truth. Walk out of the darkness and into the light. Walk out of whatever situation is holding you captive and walk into the arms of the Creator of your soul. You have the keys!

4.

DIVINE APPOINTMENTS

Have you ever had a divine appointment? If you did, were you fully aware of what was going on? Did you recognize it as it was happening? Or did it only become obvious after the fact?

A divine appointment is a "coincidence" involving God. When it happens to me, I like to say that I had a "God kiss." It's when a situation appears to be a random happening, often of no great significance at the time. Later it becomes clear that the "chance occurrence" could only have come from God.

Moses saw a burning bush. Samuel actually heard God's voice. I think they both knew right away that God was sending them a message. Signs like that are pretty hard to miss. The signs in my own life are never that obvious.

The Christian writer Warren Wiersbe felt that for the believer, everything is a divine appointment. He said there are only three possible ways a person can look at the events of life. If our situations are the result of "fate" or "chance," then our only recourse is to give up. No human can control fate or chance. If we have to try to control everything ourselves, then the situation is equally as hopeless. We just don't have that kind of power. But if God is in control, and if we trust Him to take the lead, then with his help we can handle almost anything.

One well known "divine appointment" in the Bible was between Jesus and the Samaritan woman at the well. Jesus had no apparent reason to be on that particular road in Samaria. He was separated from His apostles. There was a divine appointment He had to keep. There was someone who needed to know about Jesus from Christ himself.

God had chosen this woman, in this time and in this place, to find her eternal destiny. Her life was forever changed as a result, and through her faith, the lives of many other people were changed.

Don't ignore that little voice that tells you to take a particular road home, to stop by a certain store or to pick up the phone and make a particular phone call. You may be keeping a divine appointment that God has planned. Sometimes God may have planned a meeting between you and a total stranger. This stranger may be part of God's plan for your life.

Sometimes you are called upon to bring a message or a blessing to another person. Whatever the nature of the appointment, it holds the possibility of a wonderful, surprising and often entertaining encounter. We can then ask ourselves, "What were the chances of that?"

God loves divine appointments. He has been planning them since the beginning of time. It's His way of saying, "I love you! I'm thinking about you! You have immense value to me! You are important!"

It's like when we plan that perfect little surprise for someone we love. It gives us such a thrill to think about how much joy it will give them. That is how it must be for God when He sees us keeping the divine appointments he has arranged.

I don't know about you, but I wish those appointments could be circled in advance on my calendar. I don't want to miss a single one. They can be life savers and life changers.

Just ask the Samaritan woman. Her life was changed forever by her "chance" meeting with Jesus. With God, nothing happens by accident. His plans always have a purpose, and His purpose is always for our good and His glory.

5.

THE PRECIOUS COST OF LOVE

W ho is the one person that is most precious to you? Who is the person without whom your life would not be worth living? Who does your sun rise and set around? Who's the person that you hurry to so you can share exciting news? Who is the person who consoles you when your heart is breaking? Who would you run into a burning building to rescue? Who would you lay down your life for?

I would suspect most of us would answer these questions roughly the same way. It could be a spouse, your children or grandchildren, or maybe a dear friend. There is a thread that connects all of the people who might fall into this category. That thread is love.

Love is patient, love is kind. It does not envy, it does not boast, it is not proud. It does not dishonor others, it is not self-seeking. It is not easily angered, it keeps no record of wrongs. Love does not delight in evil but rejoices with the truth. It always protects, always trusts, always hopes, always perseveres. (1 Corinthians 13:4-7)

Honestly, I can't claim to have this kind of love for anyone on a consistent basis. I would like to think that I would enter a burning building to save my husband, my children or my grandchildren. But I am not so sure. The reason I am not sure is one of those four letter words - fear.

First John 4:18 tells us that perfect love has no fear because perfect love drives out fear. I know for a fact that my love is not perfect, because I am not perfect. Because of that imperfection I regularly experience the very human emotion of fear.

I have a great deal of fear in my life. I fear for the wellbeing of those that are the most precious to me. I fear for myself, my safety and my wellbeing. I fear all the things that I cannot control. That, my friends, is almost everything. Being a human being is like that.

Often in place of "fear" I use the word "worry." But don't be fooled. Worry is just a nicer and more acceptable word for fear. I worry because I fear a particular thing will or won't happen. At the bottom of it all, I worry that I won't get my way. And guess what? I frequently don't get my way. This life gives all of us an unhealthy dose of fear and worry.

When I think about the kind of perfect love that the Bible talks about, I think of Abraham. I am amazed by his obedience. God asked him to sacrifice his only son Isaac. This child was the most important person in his world. Isaac was the person who would be the father of a race of people who were to be as numerous as the stars.

Isaac was Abraham's reason for joy and his hope for the future. Yet Abraham trusted God and was prepared to obey Him. How could he do that? What a worrisome and fearful situation that must have been for him! Yet he carried on in perfect love for God.

We may be convinced that we could never do what Abraham was prepared to do for God. I have trouble even considering the possibility. But Abraham was different. He had an intensely personal and loving relationship with God. He believed and trusted God. He may not have known exactly what God was going to do, but he had deep faith that God would not separate him forever from his beloved son.

He knew somehow God would come through. With faith in his heart, he proceeded in obedience. God was faithful and just. He spared Isaac. He came through, just like Abraham knew He would. Abraham's experience with God was a result of his deep and abiding faith. God is always faithful and He will come through for you, too.

God loves all of His children. This was proven by the death of Jesus. He allowed His only Son to be sacrificed for us. As sinners, we could not stand blameless in front of the Holy God. It was only the sacrifice of Jesus as atonement for our sins that makes it possible for us to do so. Because we have faith in Jesus, we can stand with a clear heart before God. By Christ's sacrifice, we are forgiven and sanctified. We have received the gift of grace and salvation. We have the opportunity to spend eternity with God the Father and Jesus the Son. We have been given a precious gift of undeserved, unconditional, and unwavering love.

Perfect love can only come from a perfect God. We can't come close to loving our friends and family the way God loves us. Our love for one another here on earth will have to do for now. It's the best thing this side of heaven. Perfect love, Christ's love, will be the thing that carries us from this earth into the next life for all eternity.

6.

THE UNKNOWN IS ALWAYS KNOWN

" **A**s we trust God to give us wisdom for today's decisions, He will lead us a step at a time into what He wants us to be doing in the future." Theodore Epp

Trust is a major component in any relationship. In a healthy relationship trust goes both ways. It's extremely comforting to know someone has your back and your best interest at heart. It gives us security to know that another person loves us enough to come to our aid at any time.

But what if that someone wasn't a mere human? What if that someone was the divine God of the universe? How much safer, how much more comforted and how more secure would we feel then?

Now, glory to God, who is able, through his mighty power at work within us, to accomplish infinitely more than we might ask or think. (Ephesians 3:20)

Often when we pray, we already know how God should answer us. We have it all mapped out in our heads, the timing included. We ask God for something, then we expect Him to respond on our schedule. If God doesn't "get it done" according to our wishes and on our timetable, we become discouraged and frustrated. We begin to wonder if God is even listening to us. After a time we move on with our lives until the next crisis comes along.

The problem gets worked out, on God's time and in God's way. We may not even recognize how His hand has worked in our lives. When we do, we don't feel particularly grateful because we would have handled it a different way. Does that pretty much sum up the way prayer happens in our lives at times?

It sounds pretty selfish, I know, but it is very common. We have the tendency to pray in a very entitled manner. For some of us, it is the only time we talk to Him. God, I need this now! Help! God, I'm still waiting! Where are you?

It's sobering, or at least it should be. I have had to remind myself many times that God is not a genie in a bottle. He does not exist to obey my every command. Yes, God loves us! Yes, He wants what's best for us! Yes, He will help us in our time of need. Yes, He wants us to pray and we should believe He will answer our prayers. However, we have to understand that the answers to prayers are on His terms, not ours.

Here's the thing. God is so much better at answering our prayers in His way, in His time, and on His terms than we could ever imagine. Go ahead, pray, ask for what you need, then give it to God and stand back and let him do His thing. Prepare to be amazed! God loves to amaze us. He loves it when we smile, shake our heads and say, "Only God could have pulled that off!"

Many years ago, a man was driving his car down a busy road when the car engine began to sputter and then stalled. The driver tried to restart his car several times but had no luck. Standing on the side of the road, with the hood of his car raised, staring at his engine, a long black limousine pulled up beside him. A chauffeur got out of the front door and opened the back door of the limo. A well-dressed gentleman of obvious means stepped out of the car and offered to lend the motorist a hand.

The motorist found it difficult to believe that this rich man would have any idea what to do with an automobile engine. But, since no one else stopped to help he figured, why not? The gentleman leaned over the engine, twisted a few things, tapped a couple cables and secured a couple of plugs. He then instructed the driver to try to start the car.

The motorist was amazed when the car started. He thanked the gentlemen many times and just before the gentleman got into the back of the limo to leave, the motorist asked him his name. The gentlemen replied, "Henry Ford."

Our Maker knows what we need and when we need it. He has a plan and a purpose for our lives. We need to stay in daily communication, trust Him and be thankful.

Let Him do it His way, it is so much grander than anything we could possibly come up with.

"Never be afraid to trust an unknown future to a known God." Corrie Ten Boom

7.

HEARING VOICES

Hearing a strange voice in the still of the night is not always a bad thing. I know it sounds a little scary, but scary isn't always a bad thing either. Sometimes we need a reason to exercise our courage.

Is there a still, small voice trying to get your attention? Is it telling you something that perhaps you'd rather not hear? That still, small voice might be God. He may be asking you to change direction in your life. He may be asking you to check your position, attitude, thinking or behavior. He may be trying to change your heart, your motive, your mind, or even your whole life.

One of my favorite stories in the Old Testament is the story of Samuel. Poor little Samuel was just lying there in the temple guarding the ark of God. He was waiting for his lamp to lose its light and for sleep to come. Suddenly the course of his life was changed forever. The story of Samuel is found in 1 Samuel 3: 1-10. Here is what happened. Samuel was Eli's young assistant. Eli was advancing in age, and his eyesight was failing.

Eli was one of the great prophets of the Old Testament. But at this time of his life, Eli had lost favor with God. Eli's mistake was poor and ungodly parenting. Eli's sons were supposed to take Eli's place in the temple after his death. But God could not reward the improper upbringing of Eli's sons, so

God passed his favor to another. That favor was given to Samuel. Samuel was just a boy and I will bet no one was more surprised than Samuel himself.

One night as Samuel lay guarding the ark, he heard a voice call his name. Samuel was sure it was Eli calling him. He found Eli in his bed asleep. Samuel said, "Here I am; you called me?" Eli told him that he did not call him and told him to go back to bed. This happened two more times. By the third time, it became clear to Eli that Samuel was hearing a special voice.

Eli knew it had to be the voice of God. Once again Eli told Samuel to go back to bed, but this time he told him to listen carefully. He explained that it must be voice of God calling him. Eli told him how to answer the voice.

Samuel obeyed and listened carefully for the voice to call to him in the quiet of the night. When the voice called again, Samuel answered with the words Eli had taught him. His answer was a delight to God's ears. Samuel said, "Speak, for your servant is listening."

Can you imagine how this must have pleased God? He must have been very pleased with His decision to choose Samuel. Samuel set the bar high for all who came after him, including you and me.

How would you feel if your child answered your call with "Speak, for your servant is listening?" How about your spouse? I would guess God hears that response about as often as we do. The gift of simple obedience is rare and priceless. I adore Samuel's response to God.

God still speaks to us today, just as surely as He spoke to Samuel, Moses, Abraham and many others. The mode of communication may be different, but the voice is the same. God speaks through scripture. "All scripture is God-breathed and is useful for teaching, rebuking, correcting and training in righteousness." (2 Timothy 3:16)

God also speaks to us through our thoughts, and through our interactions with others. Have you ever been thinking and praying about something and out of the blue, an unlikely source provides an answer that clears everything up? That's God answering you.

God often speaks to us through our life experiences. Even while we are despairing of our circumstances, God may be tapping us on the shoulder to get our attention. He may want us to change something in our life and to change it soon.

The question isn't really whether God talks to us. He does. But are we willing to listen for his call? I have no doubt that God has tried to get in touch me many times and I just put the call on hold.

I have pushed that mute button many more times than I would like to admit. Sometimes I don't want to listen because I don't want to have to respond. If I did then I might have to try to explain my thoughts and actions. Sometimes I am happy being in the middle of some questionable behavior, and I simply don't want to discuss it. If I just put my hands over my ears, then maybe I won't have to change things.

At these times I'm not ready, willing or able to change. I like the results of change, but the process of change is painful. I have to get sick enough, scared enough or sorry enough to make the change happen. At that point I am finally ready to say, "Speak, for your servant is listening."

If you have come to the point in your life that you are ready to listen to a voice other than your own, I hope you will open your heart to the Lord. He is waiting to inspire your thoughts and give you a new direction. He can help change the circumstances of your life. He will help you grow and delight in the love and beauty that He has created.

Don't let God's voice be drowned out by the noise of this world. Find the quiet place inside yourself where you can hear the only voice that can guide you in the right direction. If you pay attention, God will give you the answers you desperately need.

Listen for that still small voice that is calling you in the middle of the night. May you have to courage to answer the call. May your response always be, "Speak, for your servant is listening."

8.

STAIRWAY TO HEAVEN

If you were drowning and someone tossed you a life preserver, would you reach out and grab hold of it? Would you want to be rescued? Would you want to save your life? You might be in that very situation at this moment.

Do you know the story of Jacob's ladder? In the 28th chapter of Genesis, we are told about a dream that disturbed Jacob's slumber. This dream has implications for us all.

Here's what happened. Jacob had left Beersheba and he was on his way to Harran. He stopped to rest for the night and put a stone under his head to use as a pillow. During the night he had a dream and in the dream, he saw a set of stairs. This is not the stairway in the Led Zeppelin song, at least I don't think so. These stairs connected heaven and earth. Angels were ascending and descending this ladder. At the very top of the ladder stood the Lord. God told Jacob who he was. He told him He was the same God who had blessed Abraham and Isaac.

God reaffirmed the promise made to Jacob's ancestors. The promise was that God would give Jacob and his descendants the land where Jacob was resting. God reminded Jacob that his descendants would be many. All peoples on earth were to be blessed through Jacob and his offspring. Then God said these crucial words.

I am with you and will watch over you wherever you go, and I will bring you back to this land. I will not leave you until I have done what I have promised you. (Genesis 28: 15)

We know that one of the attributes of God is that He is a promise keeper. God always keeps His word. Because of Jacob's faith, God told him He would always be with him and that He would never leave him until He had done what He promised He would do.

Do you know that God has made that same promise to us? He kept His promise to Jacob, and He will keep His promise to us as well. God brought the Israelites to the promised land. He will bring us to our promised land also.

Just as in Jacob's dream, our ladder extends all the way from earth to heaven. God provides a way for us to reach the top of the ladder and join Him in heaven for eternity.

That ladder is Jesus Christ. Whoever has faith and believes in Him will never die. Our faith is that Jesus was the Son of God. He came down to earth and took our sins upon His own back. He died for our salvation. He rose from the dead and He is seated at the right hand of the Father.

Our faith in Jesus Christ becomes the instrument that allows us to climb that ladder between heaven and earth. It gives us a way to enter heaven for all of eternity. By the power of the Holy Spirit, God lives within all of us who believe. He is always with us and He will never leave us. His home is in our hearts. He will always be with us because His spirit literally lives inside of us.

Jesus is our life preserver. He is our rescuer. His hand is the one we should grab onto when we are sinking. He will pull us through this world and into the next. He won't let us go under. He will pull us through sadness, anxiety, depression, hardship, and heartbreak.

We just need to grab His hand and hang on! Hold on when the bumps in our lives seem too hard to handle. Hold on when darkness creeps in and threatens to swallow us whole. He is waiting for us to open our eyes. He wants us to see the beauty of this world. He wants us to be with Him in heaven when our life here on earth is done.

His lifeline will pull us from the never-ending stream of problems and worries that threatens to swamp our boats. He is the shelter that will protect us when the rain comes and never seems to stop. Christ is standing on top of the flood waters, holding out His hand. He will pull us to safety. When we accept the gift of His grace, we will be brought out of the darkness and into the light.

All that glitters is not gold and we can't buy our way up the stairway to heaven. But with our faith in Jesus Christ, we can climb those stairs one step at a time. There will be angels to guide our every step and our Father is waiting for us at the top.

Won't you grab hold of the Savior's hand? Let the only one who can truly preserve your life pull you to safety, out of the reach of the troubled waters of this world. The Savior is ready, willing and able to help. Reach out and grasp His hand. He will lift you out of danger and bring you to a place of eternal safety with Him.

9.

WHAT EYES DO YOU LOOK THROUGH?

Jesus asked the blind man, "What is it you want me to do for you?" The blind man replied, "I want to see." (Luke 18:41)

Jesus didn't really have to ask. He already knew the answer to that question and everything else in the blind man's heart and mind. He knows the same about you and me.

If Jesus were to ask us that very question right this minute, what would our answer be? Would our motives be pure or self-serving? Would we ask for something that would benefit others or would we seek something for ourselves? Are we seeking to have life more abundantly, or to have more material abundance in our life? God already knows the truthful answers to those questions. The real question is this: Do we?

We can be blind in many ways. Failure to see with our eyes is just a physical defect. Spiritual blindness is a far darker thing. Don't we all want to see things more clearly? Don't we want to clearly see all the problems, and know all the answers? Wouldn't we love to be able to see the hearts, minds, and intentions of others as they truly exist? Don't we want to see the power of God, the will of God and the glory of God? God can open our eyes and our hearts so that we can see the light of His spirit at work in our lives, and in the lives of others.

John Haywood wrote, "There are none so blind as those who will not see. The most deluded people are those who choose to ignore what they already know." This reminds me what God instructed Jeremiah to tell the people of Israel. God's message was,

Listen, you foolish and senseless people with eyes that do not see and ears that do not hear. (Jeremiah 5:21)

Physical blindness is not usually something a person chooses, but spiritual blindness often is a very deliberate choice. In the passage from Jeremiah, God called out the people who had chosen not to see and hear Him. They were a senseless and foolish crowd. They knew better but they chose to disobey.

God does not want us to go through life with blinders on. God wants us to see as well with our hearts as we do with our eyes. He wants us to hear His directions crisply and clearly.

God provides us with these directions out of love. He doesn't want us to stumble around aimlessly in the dark. He invites us each day to step into the light of His protection and direction. God's desire is for us to know Him intimately and to walk closely with Him as we go through life. He longs for us to see the beauty He has created both in nature and in our fellow man.

God longs to whisper His wisdom into the ears of those who will obey without fail. His intention is for all eyes and ears to see and hear His grace and mercy. God wants nothing more than to be invited into your heart so that your spirit may feel the warm light of His love.

After giving it some honest thought, ask yourself: What is it that I want God to do for me? What is it that I want and need?

Wherever you are, whatever you are doing, there is no time to ask for what you need like the present. God is waiting to open your eyes and show you what He can do.

10.

A NEW YEAR

With the blowing of the *shofar*, another season and another year is ushered in. The Jewish New Year, Rosh Hashanah is upon us.

This is a solemn time in the Jewish faith. It is the first of the Jewish High Holy Days. The Biblical name is Yom Tervah, which literally means the day of shouting or blasting. Rosh Hashanah is also known as the Feast of Trumpets. The shofar or trumpet was an important part of Jewish ceremonies in the Old Testament and is still blown in synagogues today.

The Jewish New Year is a season of repentance. The Hebrew word for repentance is *teshuvah*. It is a time when the Jewish people celebrate the coronation of God as the King of the Universe. It is a time when they review their deeds over the past year and make amends where needed. It is a time for the rededication of faith.

I love this Jewish holiday because it is so full of meaning, hope, and tradition. Jewish traditions are absolutely beautiful in their symbolism. The Jews believe that Rosh Hashanah is a time when God reviews every aspect of their lives. It's a time of repentance and hope for the New Year ahead.

For Christians, it's a good time to examine our lives and our faith. It is a time for all of us to repent for our sins. It is a time to take a closer look at our lives and our actions and to see where we can improve as human beings and live a more pleasing life in the sight of God. It is a time for us all to recognize that God is in charge. It is a time for us all to come to the realization that God is watching over each and every one of us. We are called to remember that He has a plan and a purpose for our lives. This is a time when we can all reflect on how we can enter into a richer and more personal relationship with our Heavenly Father.

In ancient Israel, the shofar would blow to gather the people in times of celebration and to warn them in times of danger. Just as it did in ancient times, the trumpet will blow again one day to call us all together. This time the trumpet blast will signify the return of the Messiah. The King of Kings will return to judge the living and the dead. It will signify the end of this world as we know it.

A New Year is always a proper time to take stock of where we stand in our faith and in our deeds. It's a good time to ask for forgiveness and start fresh in our relationship with God. It doesn't matter if we are Jewish or Christian, the time for repentance is now. When the shofar blows on the Last Day, it will be either a time of celebration or a time of mourning, depending on where we stand with God. I pray that it's a beautiful day for you and yours. As Christians, we should never dread the coming of this day, but instead we should look forward to it with great joy.

11.

WANDERING IN THE WILDERNESS

Do you feel like you have been wandering in circles around the same situations in life? That may be exactly what you have been doing. Have the names and places in your life changed, but everything else still feels the same? Does it seem like you are condemned to go through the same series of problems, over and over?

If it seems like you are just enduring the same problems day after day and you don't seem to be getting anywhere, you may be going through a wilderness experience. Everyone has been there and there is a way out.

A wilderness experience is a period of time when we feel we are without direction. It's a dry spell spiritually. It may seem like God has been silent in our life for too long and we really don't know why. Sometimes it's because we are living outside of His will for our lives. Sometimes it's because our prayer life is in sad shape, and frankly, we haven't bothered to ask for direction. Sometimes disobedience is in our lives. Sometimes it is even unbelief.

The Israelites wandered around the desert for forty years because of their disobedience. Their trip from Egypt to the Promised Land should have only taken a few weeks. Instead they walked in circles for years because of their complaints and their disobedience. God let an entire generation die off before these people could enter the Promised Land.

Yet, God in His faithfulness kept His promise to their ancestor Abraham and brought the Israelites out of slavery. They finally reached the land of milk and honey, just as He said they would under his care.

Do not harden your hearts as you did in the rebellion, during the time of testing in the wilderness, where your ancestors tested and tried me, though for forty years they saw what I did. (Hebrews 3:8-9)

Wilderness experiences in our lives are times when we are dried up spiritually. We lack good direction. We may actually experience a sensation of thirst. Whether we realize it or not, we are craving spiritual direction. Water will not quench this thirst. We need the water of life from God.

During a wilderness experience we can look for answers in all the wrong places. Not surprisingly, when we look in the wrong places for our guidance, we may not get to where we really need to be.

We don't need to keep trudging over the same familiar ground over and over, hoping for a new outcome. God is waiting to give you a new direction for every situation in your life. He is just waiting for you to bring your life to Him. Reach out, ask God for help, and expect great things. Our God is a huge God, capable of the impossible.

I will instruct you and teach you in the way you should go; I will counsel you with my loving eye on you. Do not be like the horse or the mule, which have no understanding but must be controlled by bit and bridle or they will not come to you. (Psalm 32:8-9)

Reach out to Him. He is just waiting to place His loving arms around you and gently whisper the answers you are longing to hear.

He brought the Israelites out of the desert and into their Promised Land and He can bring you into your Promised Land as well.

12.

FLAVORFUL OR FLAVORLESS

Would you describe yourself as flavorful or flavorless? Given a choice, I think we would all like to be considered flavorful. It makes us sound like we are fun, interesting and a little whimsical. But scripture has an entirely different way of describing people who are "flavorful." The Bible tells us to be salt.

Why salt?

Jesus told his disciples to be the "salt of the earth." Remember this?

> *You are the salt of the earth; but if salt has lost its taste, how can its saltiness be restored? It is no longer good for anything, but is thrown out and trampled under people's feet. (Matthew 5:13 ESV)*

If you believe in Christ you, too, are called to be a disciple of Christ. And if you are one of His disciples, you are called upon to be salt.

What does that mean?

Salt is a versatile substance. It is used to season food, of course. It can also be used as a preservative. It was used in ancient times as a disinfectant. It was also used as a component of ceremonial offerings. It was so valuable that it was used as currency and for trade. Roman soldiers were often paid in salt.

Our bodies need salt. It helps the body send electrical signals that help regulate our kidneys and our blood pressure. It is what allows our body to become thirsty and reminds us to keep drinking the water that is essential to life. When used with care, it's good for us and it enhances the enjoyment of our food.

There are several kinds of salt. There is rock salt, sea salt, and table salt. I like to think about these different varieties. They can represent different aspects of our lives.

Take rock salt for example. A rock is a symbol of reliability and steadiness. Jesus renamed Simon, and gave him the name Peter, meaning rock. He said He would build his church "upon this rock." (Matthew 16:18) Later in the New Testament, Paul told the Corinthians that Jesus was a rock from which flowed spiritual water. (I Corinthians 10:4) These verses remind me that when I trust God I stand on a very firm foundation. It's a comforting thought.

Sea salt reminds me of water. Jesus is referred to several times as "living water" in the Bible. The most famous reference, of course, is when He referred to himself as living water when he spoke to the Samaritan Woman at the well.

Jesus answered her, "If you knew the gift of God and who it is that asks you for a drink, you would have asked him, and he would have given you living water." (John 4:10)

Table salt is the type of salt we are most familiar with. The name makes me think of a family table, a place where people come together to break bread and share the events of their day. It's a place where we connect, share laughter and make memories. We gather there for celebrations, special occasions and board games.

Jesus gathered his disciples around a table at the last supper the night before he died. Most churches have a special table in front of the altar, where communion is prepared. In heaven, those who choose Christ will gather at the table of the bridegroom's feast. The table is the gathering place of hearts, minds, and hopes.

Salt is mentioned over and over again in the Bible, both in the Old Testament and the New Testament. Salt was a symbol of friendship. Newborns were rubbed with salt at birth. This was done so that the children might be raised to have integrity and to be truthful.

Salt is a mineral of many purposes. Salt is a good thing, both by earthly standards and heavenly standards. So what does it mean to be the salt of the earth? We have been instructed by Jesus in Mark 9:50 not to lose our flavor as Christian believers. ("Salt is good, but if the salt loses its flavor, how will you season it? Have salt in yourselves, and have peace with one another.") I think that we can deduce that as believers we are to show great kindness, to be reliable, and to be honest. We are to bring the "salt of Jesus" to a thirsty world that craves love and direction. We are to have lasting bonds with friends, and fellowship with other believers. We are to flavor the world with the word of God, the Gospel.

We need to continue to grow as believers and spread the seasoning of Christ. If we lose our flavor, which is our faith, we will fail as children of God. If we will flavor the world with Christ's love and word, we will find peace with those around us. So, are you "worth your salt?"

13.

STORMS OF STRENGTH

S tormy times have a place in our lives. They make us stronger. If we are lucky, we emerge from life's tempests better able to remain upright the next time the winds of change blow and toss us about. If there were no rains, there would be no rainbows.

After the great flood, God made a covenant with mankind. He created the rainbow as a sign that the earth would never be destroyed by water again. True to God's promise, we still witness the beauty of the rainbow and the faithfulness of the covenant. Often in life, we need to experience the storm before we can enjoy the blessing.

Difficult times have a way of making us feel the need for God. We begin to realize that we are not in control. We are allowed to acknowledge our frailty and realize our deficiencies. These are opportunities for us to examine our lives and our priorities. Such times have a way of humbling us and re-establishing the priority of God in our lives.

Orson F. Whitney wrote:

No pain that we suffer, no trial that we experience is wasted. It ministers to our education, to the development of such qualities as patience, faith, fortitude, and humility. All that we suffer and all that we endure, especially when we endure it patiently, builds up our characters, purifies our hearts, expands our souls and makes us more tender and charitable, more worthy to be called the children of God...and it is through sorrow and suffering, toil and tribulation, that we gain the education that we came here to acquire.

We were born to learn how to love God. Learning to love with our whole heart can be painful. But nothing that comes without pain is worth much in our hearts and lives. Pain promotes growth and growth has its individual rewards. To bloom into the people we were created to be, we need the rain along with the sunshine. Below is a little story that gives me hope whenever storms blow through my life.

The Young Tree

The small tree faced many storms through its young life. It faced powerful winds, torrential rains, seasons of heat and drought. In winter, snow and ice would lie heavy across its branches. At times the young tree questioned its Maker asking, "Why have you let so many storms come into my life?" His Maker whispered, "You will understand one day, but for now, stand firm, and you will make it through the storms. The challenges will pass, if you stay faithful and strong." The tree fretted. "If I go through one more hard winter, I fear the snow and ice will break my branches. If I must face more powerful winds I will be uprooted and blown away." His Maker whispered, "Stand strong, dig your roots deep into the soil, and you will understand someday." The young tree kept these thoughts in his heart and grew ever stronger as it faced its challenges. In the toughest of times, it found a way to stand firm and survive through the worst of storms. As the young tree grew taller, stronger and fully mature, the tree realized it was the storms of life that had made it stronger. ~ *Greta Dsouza*

As you go through the storms of life, stand firm in your faith in God. Grow stronger in your knowledge of the word of God. Let your roots grow deep and firm. Let yourself become fully grown despite the wind and the rain. You will feel His faithful hand keeping you steady as you wade through the storm waters. He will keep you safe no matter how high the waters rise.

14.

GOD KISSES

I can hear you asking yourself right now, what is a God Kiss? It's that moment when you realize that you and God have just experienced a sweet moment in time together. It is a time for just you and Him.

You know those times when you are thinking about something that only you and God know about? Perhaps thoughts have been swirling around in your head that no one else knows about. They aren't necessarily profound thoughts. They can be silly observations or just a saying that has touched your heart. Maybe you heard something that sparked an idea or piqued your interest. Then, out of the blue, someone says something that touches on that exact same thought.

At that moment, you know that God has heard you and is listening to you. Whatever it is, even if it is silly nonsense, God is interested. That's when the awe washes over you. You realize that out of all the people in the world, and all the problems that exist, the God of this universe cares about you and knows your most intimate thoughts. He not only wants to be a part of your life, but He wants you to know that every aspect of your life has value to Him. That is what I call a kiss from God.

Your eyes saw my unformed body; all the days ordained for me were written in your book before one of them came to be. How precious to me are your thoughts, God! How vast is the sum of them! (Psalm 139:16-17)

It's the nature of a close relationship. We all have friends in our life with whom we are extremely close. Some people know us so well that they often know exactly what we are thinking. We have shared so many experiences and talked so frequently with our friend that our minds go to the same place at the same time. You not only know what the other is thinking, you know how they feel deep inside. You share a close bond, a connection. You have a real and deep relationship.

What a sweet and special bond of love and friendship! That is what God wants to have with us. He wants to be the one we share our dreams, hopes, and thoughts with. He wants to share our joys and sorrows. He wants us to feel His comfort, peace, and presence in every moment and in every situation. He wants us to crave time alone with Him like we do our family and friends. He is our Heavenly Father, our creator and our very best friend.

How fortunate are we to have a best friend that holds all power in heaven and on earth! With a friend like that, why wouldn't we make it priority to spend time with Him every day?

A God kiss is priceless. A God kiss is God's breath touching our cheek, inhaling our essence, whispering words of love in our ear.

May you feel the softness of His touch upon you. May you feel the warmth of His kiss and know the pleasure of His closeness. May you draw comfort from His love and His desire to be near to you. May your heart draw near to Him, near enough to feel His kiss.

15.

HOPE IS ETERNAL

Do you know what causes some of the greatest despair among Christians? For many it is the worry and fear they have about loved ones who have not accepted Christ.

At the countless number of conferences, prayer meetings, and Bible Studies I have attended, the subject frequently comes up. When it does, there is a heaviness in the air, as each person considers the spiritual status of family and friends. The uncertainty can be heartbreaking. We shed tears at the thought of a loved one spending eternity in darkness.

The idea is unimaginable. The thought of a loved one spending eternity in hell is more than one can bear. An oppressive feeling of oppression weighs on the heart and sickens the stomach. There are no words to describe that bleakness. If you are in that situation, I would like to give you some hope.

Most of us are familiar with C.S. Lewis, probably the greatest Christian apologist in the Twentieth Century. C. S. Lewis's faith was a work in progress. In fact, Lewis's starting point may have been more extreme than most peoples. Lewis tried atheism, naturalism, determinism and even dabbled in the occult before he became a Christian. His road to faith was a process. After doubting for many years, he finally came to believe in the possibility of a universal God. The process did not stop there. Eventually Lewis came to believe and have faith in Jesus Christ.

God courted Lewis's mind and heart in a way that led him to understanding and faith. He arrived at the only conclusion that made sense to his analytical mind. Despite his years of unbelief, he finally had to give himself to the idea that Jesus was indeed the Christ, the Son of God, the Savior promised by the Father.

C.S. Lewis had his own unique path to walk. But we all walk a unique path. All our paths are different. Some of our paths have huge peaks and valleys. Other paths are smooth and level. What we find along the way is placed there by God. There is a reason for each pothole. God alone knows what lies along our road. Our journeys are as individual as our fingerprints.

God's love transforms hearts. It happened to Paul in the First Century, and it happened to C.S. Lewis in the Twentieth Century. We know a lot about them because they both made great contributions to spreading the Gospel. But this transformation happens constantly, hundreds and thousands of times a day somewhere in the world. Lives that lived in darkness are constantly coming to the light.

Surely God can change the heart of your loved ones and mine. What can we do to help? We need to keep praying and trust God. Don't stop. Don't slow down. Invite change but don't try to force it to happen. Let God be in charge.

We are called to be a model of Christ's love in their lives. They need to witness our faith in action. If you don't believe your progress is being noticed by your loved ones, you are sadly mistaken. Your actions speak louder than any megaphone ever invented.

Walk your path in prayer and hope. Trust and believe in God. He wants salvation for your loved ones much more than you can imagine. They are His children too. He wants them in heaven with Him one day and He will do everything divinely possible to make sure that happens. He is the God of seemingly impossible situations.

What is impossible with man, is possible with God. (Luke 18:27)

Remember that God will never fail to complete the work of salvation that He has begun in a person's life. We must continue to hope. We can understand this verse with our minds, but we have to live it in our hearts. Jesus came for our salvation, not our damnation.

Be confident of this, that He who began a good work in you will carry it on until the day of Christ Jesus. (Philippians 1:6)

The Christian author and speaker Beth Moore says,

I have no few regrets in life. I was pretty messed up and my path was strewn with poor decisions. But I've never regretted a single second with Jesus, a single decision made in His name, a single time I chose His will over mine, a single hour I spent in Scripture. He is unregrettable.

This statement spoke to my heart. I hope it speaks to yours also. I firmly believe that if we continue to pray for our loved ones and never lose hope, God will take care of the rest.

16.

WE CAN'T GO BOTH WAYS

Are you old enough to remember when the Wizard of Oz came on TV once a year? When I was a child it was always a special event. Nothing else was quite like it.

Remember the scene where Dorothy first met the Scarecrow? She had come to a crossroad. The Yellow Brick Road went right, left, and straight ahead. One path led to the Emerald City, but which one? She hears a voice that says "Pardon me but that way is a very nice way to go." She notices a scarecrow in a nearby cornfield who seems to be pointing to his left. She is confused until he says, "It's pleasant down that way too," and points to his right.

Now she is really confused. To top it off, the Scarecrow then crosses his arms and points in both directions. He says, "Of course people do go both ways!" Now she is pretty sure that he is the one speaking to her.

The absurdity of the solution he proposes is clear. Even though one person may turn left, and another person may turn right, one person cannot go down both roads at the same time. One person cannot go "both ways."

The Scarecrow has given Dorothy an easy (and confusing) answer to a tough problem. He seems to have a hard time making a decision so he would prefer to have things both ways. We do this in our lives as well. When faced with difficult decisions we want to avoid making hard choices. But when we are faced with major decisions, "going both ways" is usually not possible. We have to choose one particular path and follow it. At that point we have to leave the other possible paths behind us.

Most people are searching for direction. The best way to find the solution is to stop long enough to talk to and then listen to God. When we are still long enough to listen with our hearts we can begin to find answers. There are countless choices in our lives, and everyone else seems to have advice for us. The distractions of everyday life are often what prevent us from focusing on the solution to our problems. Indecision can hang over us like a thick fog of the mind. It clouds our thinking and keeps us from moving forward. How do we find the right path on our yellow brick road? The one that leads us to the streets paved in gold. PRAYER!

King David had this exact problem many times. In desperation, he called out to God.

Show me the right path, O Lord; point out the road for me to follow. Lead me by your truth and teach me, for you are the God who saves me. All day long I put my hope in you. (Psalm 25:4-5 NLT)

God saved David from King Saul who sought to take his life. David had faith that God would guide him and show him the right path. He knew that God would guide him and stand beside him along the way. His faith in a loving God gave him the security and peace he needed in order to make the decisions necessary to follow God's plan for his life. God is faithful to those who trust him.

The Lord is good and does what is right; he shows the proper path to those who go astray. He leads the humble in doing right, teaching them his way. The Lord leads with unfailing love and faithfulness all who keep his covenant and obey his demands. (Psalm 25:8-10 NLT)

God is waiting to help us too. Whatever you are struggling with, go to God. Whatever seems insurmountable in your life, go to God. Whatever is causing you pain and holding you mentally hostage, go to God. He is ready, willing and able to address the problems and concerns in your life. He is waiting for you to put them in His hands. Bring your concerns to Him with faith and trust.

Then be patient. God's timetable is not the same as ours. But His answers are perfect answers. His ways are perfect ways.

Don't be afraid to trust. Trust can be hard, but it is necessary. Pray for strength as you await God's answers. He will always guide you through your most troublesome situations.

Dorothy finally realized that there is "no place like home." God hopes that each of us will find our way home to Him. The road that leads us back to Him is Jesus. The navigational tool is prayer. The fuel is faith and trust.

May we all meet the loving and powerful God that stands behind the curtain of space and time. He is waiting to bring His faithful servants home to live for eternity with Him. How wonderful it will be when we are finally reunited with the Father in heaven, and once again see our departed loved ones who have gone before us. Trust in Him. He will take us by the hand and lead us home.

17.

THE SWEETEST WORD

The sweetest word in our language is "grace." In English, grace means the free and unmerited favor of God, manifested in the salvation of sinners and the bestowing of blessings.

The word "grace" is derived from the Latin word *gratia*. The Latin word has many shades of meaning. To the ancients, the word meant favor, good will, kindness and friendship. In the right context it could mean gratitude and as a word of thanks. The Spanish word "gracias" is a direct descendant of the word used by the Romans.

The concept of "grace" is even older. In the Old Testament the word most often used was *chesed*. Again, we have a word that does not translate easily into English. This was the problem facing the 16th century Bible scholar Miles Coverdale when he translated the Psalms and other parts of the Bible.

Coverdale found the word so difficult to express in English that he invented a brand-new word to convey the meaning. The word was "lovingkindness."

"Lovingkindness" appeared 23 times in his translation of the Psalms alone. In other parts of the Old Testament he found the word best translated into words like mercy, goodness and favor. Most of the time it reflected God's special attitude towards his covenant people - Israel.

God's lovingkindness is that sure love which will not let Israel go. Not all Israel's persistent waywardness could ever destroy it. Though Israel be faithless, yet God remains faithful still. This steady, persistent refusal of God to wash his hands of wayward Israel is the essential meaning of the Hebrew word. ... The loving-kindness of God towards Israel is therefore wholly undeserved on Israel's part. N.H. Snaith, Distinctive Ideas of the Old Testament, London (1944).

A perfect example is the story of Moses and how he led the Israelites out of Egypt. God guided the Israelites daily during the Exodus from Egypt and during the next forty years they wandered in the desert. Eventually God led them to the Promised Land. He forgave them time after time for their behavior during the journey. They were disobedient. They grumbled and complained. Yet He preserved His people and enabled them to persevere.

When we read Exodus, we can witness God's frustration with His chosen people. In today's vernacular, they pushed all of His buttons and got on His very last nerve. The patience, mercy, and lovingkindness that God showed Israel was definitely what we call "grace." It was a gift of undeserved forgiveness given out of love and steadfastness, given by a God who keeps His promises. He held up His end of the bargain with Israel, even when they went far astray.

In the New Testament there is a different but similar word that describes God's attitude toward man. It is the Greek word *charis*.

The New Testament brings God's grace into action by the death of Jesus on the cross. God came down from heaven in human form and changed the history of the earth forever by dying on the cross. By rising from the dead on the third day, He sealed our undeserved forgiveness, and granted all believers salvation in heaven with Him for eternity.

18.

WHO IS YOUR KING?

S top for a moment and ask yourself a few questions. Where do I devote most of my resources? What do I think about the most? How do I spend most of my energy? What do I value most in life?

These are important questions. We should all contemplate the answers we come up with. It's a way to figure out who or what is the King of our lives. Whatever or whoever you give your biggest share of your thoughts, time and talents to - that is your king. It's a question only you can honestly answer.

Life has a way of getting so busy and hectic that it's easy to let our priorities get out of balance. It happens before we know it. Generally something unpleasant has to take place before we are forced to stop and account for ourselves. At that point it is a good idea to take time to figure out where we are and why things have taken us off the path of God's will.

In Israel's history, during the time of the Judges, the people did not have an earthly king. They thought that this was the cause of all their troubles. All the countries around them had kings, and perhaps they felt a little left out. Or perhaps they were dissatisfied with God's leadership and wanted a human king to take the reins.

We have all heard it said, "Be careful what you wish for." God gave them their desire. Their best thinking was to reject God in favor of a mortal, sinful human king. This was a bad decision for the people of Israel. It was the beginning of a long line of cruel monarchs who ruled unwisely over them. The people made a very poor choice, but God gave them what they wanted and let them find out for themselves.

Are the choices we make today any better? We have tremendous freedom in our lives. We choose what we eat, where we work, how we spend our money, where we worship and what we worship. Do we fully comprehend the importance of that last bit? I am not sure that we do. We must realize that the king of our lives is the thing we worship above all else. The last part of that last sentence is the most critical. I am convinced that we fail to realize what occupies the highest position in our lives. Whatever we spend the majority of our time thinking about and striving for, that is our king.

God will never force Himself on anyone for any reason. He has given us free will so that we may freely choose Him, desire Him, love Him and serve Him. Nobody wants love that is not freely given. God allows us to choose our King and He allows us to feel the consequences of our decisions. The Israelites found that out.

Wisdom requires us to stop and evaluate our priorities from time to time. It's easy to get off course. When we do, we can become slaves to the material world. Are we caught up in craving for more things, more wealth, a bigger house, a newer car, and all the other trappings of the material world? Are we seeking to keep up with the Joneses? Are we striving for acceptance at work, in a social group, or in our family? Are bad habits getting out of hand? Are these yearnings causing problems in our lives?

If our answer is yes, we may need to stop in our tracks and re-evaluate. The king we have placed over our lives may not be the one we need to be truly happy. Perhaps God is the One who should be in charge.

God will never leave His people, but His people leave Him all the time. We all know that if we do not learn from history, history will repeat itself. There is a reason Israel's struggles are described in the Bible in such great detail. We are told about their story so we can learn from their mistakes.

Over time the things that have enslaved mankind have changed. But the outcome remains the same. Whatever we have chosen to replace God in our lives will have serious consequences in our lives. Ordinary kings bring us bondage. But the King of Kings will set us free.

Who or what do you need to be set free from? There is only One who can be counted on to break that bondage. Call on Him today. He is waiting for us to make the right choice. Choose liberation over bondage. The thief comes only to steal and kill and destroy.

I came that they may have life and have it abundantly. (John 10:10 ESV)

19.

METAMORPHOSIS

W e live in a chrysalis. Our lives are always in a transitional state.

When a caterpillar becomes large enough, it spins itself into a silky cocoon known as a chrysalis. Inside, it is transformed into a beautiful butterfly. People undergo a similar process in their lives. The transformation in man is not only physical but also spiritual, mental and emotional.

Our bodies act as a chrysalis for us from birth until death. We continually grow and mature. First, we are babies, then children, then teenagers, then adults. As adults, we continue to grow as we grow older. The final change is the experience of death.

Our lives are a series of physical changes. But it is not just our physical bodies that change. As we go through life we also go through changes in all aspects of our life. Life itself is a process of constant change.

A physician studies changes to our physical bodies. A psychologist studies the ways that our mental and emotional status changes and develops. Theologians study the spiritual changes that take place in man. All of them find the study of such things gives them deeper insight into life. They see the changes that benefit us, and the changes that are harmful for us.

As a follower and student of Christ, I find spiritual transformations fascinating. There is nothing more interesting than the story of how a human life changes when it finds God.

When I first became a Christian, I knew nothing about having an intimate relationship with Jesus. Everything I knew about God I learned by growing up in a Catholic household and attending parochial schools. It was a good foundation. But for me, it wasn't nearly enough. I could not see the path that God had planned for me.

Like most young people, I spent my teens and early twenties living life as I saw fit. I seldom thought about the consequences of my behavior until it was too late. After a series of pretty terrible choices, I realized that I needed God to guide my life. I wasn't doing so well on my own.

I started craving more time with the Lord. I began to seek out other believers to spend time with. Every part of my life came under spiritual scrutiny. Slowly, layers of misguided thinking and questionable habits were peeled away from my life. Some things took a very long time.

Physically I am a mature adult. Spiritually I am still in the chrysalis, still undergoing change. I have so much more to learn concerning God, my life and my relationships with my fellow human beings. The process is in the journey. Some days I learn well, and I advance in my spiritual maturation. Other days I fail. Always, I try again the next day to make progress in my development as a child of God.

If God can take something as ordinary as a caterpillar and change it into an exquisitely beautiful butterfly, I am sure He can transform my willing heart into something better. My heart longs to please Him, learn His ways, and grow in love.

Every day I transition a little bit. Most of the time the change is positive, but not always. Life is like that. I have moments of inspiration and clarity. I also have moments of setbacks and pain. I accept it all as part of the process.

Do not conform to the pattern of this world, but be transformed by the renewing of your mind. Then you will be able to test and approve what God's will is--his good, pleasing and perfect will. (Romans 12:2)

It's OK if we have days in our lives when we feel we haven't made much of a change in ourselves or the lives of others. The most important thing is to keep our eyes focused on Christ. We give Him our lives and let Him be in control of our growth and change. Every day is a new day and a new experience. Every day we can grow into the person God created us to be. If we live and grow in faith, we will undergo a tremendous metamorphosis. Our lives will possess a beauty that can only be imagined in the mind of God.

And I will give you a new heart, and I will put a new spirit in you. I will take out your stony, stubborn heart and give you a tender, responsive heart. (Ezekiel 36:26)

The Bible says that our unique beauty will emerge from our hearts for all to see. We are being formed by the very hand of God. That gives me hope for this life and for the prospect of life in eternity. Though I am an imperfect human now, I believe that one day I will become a perfect child of God. I may have to wait for my life in heaven to reach perfection. But one day, if I continue to love and serve God, I have faith that I will finally emerge from my chrysalis into the light and the presence of Christ. I wait for that day in joyous anticipation.

20.

NO PAIN, NO GAIN

The teachable times in our lives are often very hard times. These are the times in our lives that we realize that something must change. The pain gives us the motivation we need to be open minded to change. The outcome of those times determines the path and the extent of our spiritual growth.

When we are babies, we must first learn to drink milk. Some of us catch on right away, and some of us need to try over and over before we finally learn how to take nourishment into our bodies. It is a strange new world. We grow a little every day. We rapidly acquire new skills. There is so much to learn during the first few years of our lives. Each new task builds upon the last and we are required to use different parts of our bodies and our minds. We don't understand at the time how our bodies and minds are growing and learning.

Each time an infant kicks his legs he is growing and changing. He is building muscles. The strength that he acquires through this hard work will one day lead him to walk upright, and before long he can run. Every part of the human body is designed to grow and learn in this way.

We grow in our behavioral aspects as well. We are taught concept after concept by our parents. We are rewarded for good behavior and our bad behavior is corrected. We quickly learn the meaning of the word "NO!" Little ones hear that word so often that it can become one of their favorite words. "No!" becomes their answer to almost everything. It's easy to say and it carries just the right amount of authority. It lets them feel like they are in charge. Unfortunately, they often are. It takes strength and steadiness to stand up to the whims of a toddler. It takes discipline and wisdom to turn tantrums around and it takes patience to make those times into teachable moments.

Young animals in the wild usually don't have the luxury of safe teachable moments. Much of the times these crucial moments involve life or death situations. For example, young meerkats must learn to eat scorpions. When they are very young, adults bring dead scorpions to them. But as they get older, they must learn to hunt the live ones in order to get enough to eat. A mistake can mean disaster.

Eagles teach their young to fly by pushing them out of the nest. If they fall too far, their mother swoops down and catches them and returns them to the nest. This is how they build the strength and confidence they need to in order to learn to fly.

The same sort of thing happens with our spiritual growth when we first accept God in our lives. Beginning Christians are attracted to God and make a decision to follow Him. It may not always seem like it, but they are under the spiritual protection of God. They undergo trials of faith. They experience hard times. But they are always under the loving protection of God. He protects them from trials they are not ready to handle. We learn to trust his guidance. In doing so we become stronger in our faith.

Now may the God of peace, who through the blood of the eternal covenant brought back from the dead our Lord Jesus, that Shepherd of the sheep, equip you with everything good for doing his will, and may he work in us what is pleasing to him, through Jesus Christ, to who be glory forever and ever. (Hebrews 13:20-21)

Our good and patient God would never give us anything before He knew we were ready to handle it and learn, spiritually, physically, mentally and emotionally. He may use hard times as lessons to teach us the right way to live life. But He will never give up on us in any situation. Our spiritual and physical lives depend on His authority and strength. That is what carries us forward.

God is consistent and faithful. We are the ones that doubt. We are the ones that go to the edge of the nest, kicking, and screaming. We would be content to stay where everything feels safe, even though the plain fact is that we must grow stronger to survive. We cannot do that in the nest.

We may be under the delusion that if God is working in our lives, then every moment should be happy and comfortable. Not so! Growing up is hard. Sometimes it hurts. That is the reality of life. Life is supposed to hurt, and it is supposed to be hard. Growing pains are a real thing. No one is exempt from potholes in the road of life.

If the eagle fails to develop his wings, he won't be able to fly. If a meerkat doesn't learn to eat scorpions safely, he won't get enough to eat. If a baby doesn't develop his legs he won't learn to walk and run. And if we fail to work our way through spiritual difficulties, our faith in God cannot grow strong.

Jesus said,

> *You don't have enough faith. I tell you the truth, if you had faith even as small as a mustard seed, you could say to this mountain, "Move from here to there," and it would move. Nothing would be impossible. (Matthew 17:20 NLT)*

There is always a certain amount of pain that goes along with any growth. That is the way life is for everyone. It's hard at the time, but there is a reward for every growing pain. Let's not fear the pain. Instead, let's be afraid if there isn't any pain.

We can expect some pain to be there in every teachable moment in our lives. One day we will soar with the eagles.

He will cover you with his feathers, and under his wings, you will find refuge. (Psalm 91:4)

21.

NO NANA! NOT THE CAR WASH!

Not long ago I was in Indiana on Nana duty, helping to take care of my two-year-old grandson. I needed to get my car washed while I was there. Since I was pressed for time, the only way that was going to happen was if I took him with me to the car wash. What an adventure!

I knew he had never been through a car wash. Before we went, I tried to prepare him for what was going to happen. I figured if he had some idea of the process, he would not be afraid. I told him we were going to drive through a big car scrubbing machine. I told him we would stay in the car while everything happened, and I told him we would be perfectly safe. I told about the big brushes, and about the big mops that would go back and forth over the car. I told him about the soap suds and the sprays of water that would rinse off the car.

I explained that it would be a great adventure. He sounded excited and he seemed to be a willing participant. He was doing great right up until the end.

Then something happened I had forgotten about. The huge noisy fans that dry off the car kicked in. The force of the wind rocked the car back and forth. He was not prepared for that.

As soon as those fans began to blow, a sweet little hand went up in the back seat desperately searching for reassurance. He needed to know that Nana was still there and that he was going to be fine. Fearful tears began to flow. I took his hand and offered as much comfort as I could.

Good job Nana! Way to scare a child! I realized too late that I had forgotten to give him all the information that he needed in order to go through the car wash without fear. My failure to give him the complete information left him vulnerable to a surprise experience. Thank goodness Chick Fil A was right next door. A small bag of french fries goes a long way towards fixing things.

After all the tears were dried, I thought over the experience. We are all exactly like this little boy. When we know what to expect in life, we can handle things pretty well. But sometimes things don't follow the script. We feel the same way he did when the fans kicked on. We are scared and feel alone. We search for loving arms to hold us and a strong hand to guide us. We don't like being uninformed and thrown for a loop. We like to know what is coming and how to prepare.

The most loving thing we can do for those we care about is to help them understand what they need to know to prepare them for the inevitable car washes of life. We can give them the information they need to prepare for new things in life. If we do our job well, we can also prepare them for life in the world to come.

We are never alone. We don't have to fight the scary things in this world on our own.

Be strong and courageous. Do not be afraid; do not be discouraged, for the Lord your God will be with you wherever you go. (Joshua 1:9)

Thank goodness that our Heavenly Father loves us enough to tell us everything we need to know. He gives us the information we need to walk through life. He gave us the Bible to teach us his laws. He sent His only Son Jesus to hold our hands and give us comfort and security for eternity. If we are believers, we are never alone in any storm in life.

By the grace of the Father and the death and resurrection of Jesus, forgiveness has been granted. We have His word that if we accept Christ as our Lord and Savior then we will never have to fear anything that may threaten us in life. Many times, we face great storms full of loud noises that cower us and make us feel vulnerable. God tells us that no matter what happens we will sit with Him at the great banquet table in heaven. There we will feast together in celebration of His faithfulness and love for eternity. There will be nothing there to scare us.

By the way, I have it on good authority that our reward in Heaven will be far more satisfying than a small bag of french fries. It will be the glory of eternal life with God. But between you and me, I do hope french fries are included. I don't think heaven would be complete without them.

22.

AGE IS THE COST OF WISDOM

I am part of the aging baby boomer generation. I'm the part of the generation that is more boomer than baby. But there is an upside to that. With age comes wisdom.

When most people try to picture God, they imagine a person who is very old, with wavy white hair and a long white beard. Painters and sculptors throughout the ages have shown God in this way. But where does the imagery come from? I think most people expect someone as wise as God to be old. In our minds, old age holds with it the promise of wisdom. And many times, that is correct. But not always.

Where does this wisdom come from? Why does age seem to symbolize wisdom? It's not hard to figure out. A person who has lived a long life has had years of experience dealing with life. The Bible has lots of advice from those in their golden years. Why? In one word – experience.

In life, there are two things that you can be sure of, a constant series of changes and a great deal of experience gained from going through those changes. The longer we live, the more things seem to change. Change is hard. Learning how to accept and to adapt to change is the basis of all wisdom.

Some changes are good and wonderful and make us downright euphoric. Others are heartbreaking, mind-numbing and paralyzing. Every one is a learning opportunity.

Sometimes we see the lesson right away. Other times we are at a loss, and we wish there wasn't so much change in our lives. No matter how we view change, there is the prospect of growth. If we accept it and deal with it, it is not so bad. If we fight it and fail to understand it, we have a lot of pain. Either way, the fires of change will temper our lives and burn away the dross. We will become stronger. God in His infinite wisdom always works for the greater good in the lives of those He loves.

And we know that in all things God works for the good of those who love him, who have been called according to his purpose. (Romans 8:28)

I have been giving a great deal of thought to age and wisdom lately. I can honestly say that in many things I have gained knowledge and perspective as I have gotten older. I have had to go through some pretty hard and hurtful times in my life to get where I am today. I am not perfect by any means, but I do like myself a lot better.

When I look back over the years, I can see just how much I have changed. Like most of us, I have some cringe-worthy memories of crazy things I did. I have regrets about the kind of person I was. Today I am at peace with my past because those experiences helped change me into the person I am today. I sincerely hope that the changes I have gone through in my life will help me inspire you to grow in your faith. True faith brings about transformation.

Recently I was in Indiana with my grandson while his parents attended a wedding out of state. Nothing will make you feel your age more than trying to keep up with a two-year-old. He was in constant motion. During this visit, I took him to Chick Fil A for lunch. He loves to play on the equipment they have for kids in a section of the restaurant.

Inside the play area there are benches where the adults sit. It became very obvious to me that these were the Grandma benches. The mothers were sitting in the main restaurant, lunching and talking and trying to get in a bit of girlfriend time. They were seeking a few minutes of peace. We Grandmas were the guardians of the play place. I came to two very startling realizations. One, I had graduated from the moms' table to the Grandma bench. Two, I wasn't the nice Grandma I thought I was. I wasn't smiling and calling everyone sweetie and honey as I gently corrected the little darlings.

Nope. I was the bossy one saying things like, "Hey, Hey, HEY you in the flowered pants – slow down! GIRLS, GIRLS, stop screaming! What is it with all the screaming? You have to follow the rules! You are going the wrong way on the slide – don't walk up it, go down it!"

When did I stop being the rule breaker and start being the rule enforcer? When I was young, rules only applied to other people. When did they start applying to me? And when did I start being the play place boss?

Perhaps over the years I have obtained some wisdom. Lord knows I have prayed for it often enough. God gives us constant reassurance.

If you need wisdom, ask our generous God, and he will give it to you. He will not rebuke you for asking. (James 1:5 NLT)

Thank you, God!

23.

MY FATHER'S EYES

The most beautiful soul is a sympathetic soul. The most beautiful heart is a compassionate heart. The most beautiful eyes are caring eyes. The most desirable friend is a friend that listens to you with all their heart. If you have someone like this in your life you know you have found a rare and valuable jewel.

Many years ago, there was a Christian song that had the verse, "She has her Father's eyes." The Father, of course, was God. I have thought of that song many times. What does it mean to have our Father's eyes? Can we learn to look at others through our Father's eyes?

What would such eyes look like? I think such eyes would shine with a great number of qualities: Empathy, care, concern, sensitivity, warmth, love, tenderness, mercy, leniency, tolerance, kindness, humanity and charity. Do you know someone like that?

I have been blessed with some pretty remarkable people in my life. Many of them simply radiate these qualities. Of course, it is hard to display all these characteristics consistently. Most of us do well if we have these gifts when we are at the top of our game. But some carry these blessings in the depth of their heart, and they shine brightly in both good and bad times.

I have only seen all of these in a set of eyes once in my life and I will never forget them. I am convinced I saw the eyes of Jesus.

My family and I were on vacation in Washington DC. We were walking down a sidewalk heading back to our hotel after playing tourist all day. We stopped at a crosswalk, waiting for the light to change so we could cross the street.

For some reason, I turned around. There on the sidewalk sat a man who was down and out. He was accepting money from anyone who would help, and he was obviously a man who needed help from his fellow man. I am not what you would call a "soft touch." My natural tendency is to be skeptical in such situations. How do I know what the money I give will be used for?

More times than I care to admit I have simply walked past such people with scarcely a second thought. But this encounter was different. I was drawn to this man. It was as if there was a gravitational pull on my soul. Everything slowed down. I reached into my wallet, found a few dollars, and walked over to him. My eyes were fixed on his and time seemed to stop for just an instant.

In that moment, I knew that I was looking into eyes of our Lord. The entire world was reflected in his eyes. We held one another's gaze for what seemed like a long time. I felt that he saw completely through me, and I felt I saw a deep well of holiness down inside him. Without breaking eye contact he said to me, "God bless you." I have never experienced anything like that in my life. His eyes have haunted me ever since.

Was this really a holy man? Or was God using a very ordinary man to touch my heart and teach me a lesson in compassion? I can't tell you. I know God places people in my life at the most unexpected times to teach me about Him.

Regardless of the facts, the deep and abiding truth was that for that moment, God spoke to me. My heart was captivated by the eyes of my Father in heaven.

The greatest compliment I could receive would be to tell me that I had my Father's eyes. I think every day about compassion. I know that for me compassion happens more easily in certain circumstances, for specific reasons, and in response to specific people. Too much of the time it just does not arise in me the way I am sure God wants it to.

The ability to consistently view everyone with the same level of compassion would be quite a gift. I'm not sure it is possible for a human being to have such a gift. As sinful creatures we place conditions on the love we give. We have a hard time finding empathy for those we disagree with, to those who live in ways we disagree with, and those who are poor and destitute. We pick and choose the subjects of our generosity.

I don't think that God operates this way. I think God's love is universal. I think that His love is like rain - it falls on the just and the unjust alike. It is what we do with His outpouring of love that makes all the difference.

I have a long way to go before I can bear even a slight resemblance to my Father and His beautiful eyes of compassion. How about you? Is there at least a family resemblance?

24.

THE TOWER OF APPLE

Have you seen the billboards that purport to speak in God's voice? My favorite is the one that says in the familiar voice of a frustrated parent, "Don't make me come down there!"

This billboard made me think about the Tower of Babel. Do you remember the story? It is a story about the aspirations and the arrogance of human beings in relation to their Creator.

The story of the Tower of Babel is in the 11th chapter of Genesis. There we read the story of Noah's descendants. They were all living as a community that was fast becoming a city. In the midst of this city, they decided to build a tower made of bricks. It was to be so tall that the top of the tower would be in heaven. Their stated purpose was to make a name for themselves so they would not be scattered across the earth.

The Lord said,

> *"If as one people speaking the same language, they have begun to do this, then nothing they plan to do will be impossible for them. Come, let us go down and confuse their language so they will not understand each other." So, the Lord scattered them from there over all the earth, and they stopped building the city. That is why it was called Babel—because there the Lord confused the language of the whole world. From there the Lord*

scattered them over the face of the whole earth. (Genesis 11:6-8)

And so it has been. At least that's the way things have been so far.

Think how far technology has come in the last fifty years. Today, almost everyone in developed countries has a personal computer in their home. Most everyone has a smartphone. The smartphones of today contain more power and technology than the computers that guided the astronauts on their voyage to the moon.

Now think about the apps that are available for your smart phones and computers. Translation applications are used all over the world. They enable people to talk to any other people in the world with only the computer as an interpreter. Are we closing the gap opened by God when he scattered the peoples across the earth?

In an article written by Vanessa Bates Ramirez a while back, she stated: "Google has developed deep learning software that can accurately translate sentences from one language to another, but there are still many nuances of language that only a human brain can grasp."

You see, slang, colloquialisms and idioms are still very hard for computers to accurately translate. There are a variety of sounds and ideas that exist in one language and not in another. That makes consistent and faithful translation a little tough. As time goes on, I have little doubt that these problems will be solved and very little will be "lost in translation."

Is history about to repeat itself? I am reminded of children at play. You can take a toy from them because it might be harmful to them. Then when you turn around you find that they have found something else to play with that does the same exact thing. It is a constant struggle to keep them safe. Is that what humans are like? Are we just as stubborn as these children?

God was not pleased with the arrogance of the people who thought they could reach heaven on their own. He put an end to their delusions with one swift stroke. Is there a lesson here for us? I think the message of the story is this: We have never been so self-reliant that we have no need for God.

Our self-sufficiency is illusory. We have made great strides in technology. These leaps forward are seen in medicine, communications and research. But no matter how advanced we become we will never catch up with God. We can't even come close. It's like trying to teach a toddler advanced calculus. It just can't be done. And it is arrogant of us to think otherwise.

"The moment you have a self at all, there is a possibility of putting yourself first – wanting to be the centre – wanting to be God, in fact. That was the sin of Satan: and that was the sin he taught the human race. Some people think the fall of man had something to do with sex, but that is a mistake....what Satan put into the heads of our remote ancestors was the idea that they 'could be like Gods' – could set up on their own as if they had created themselves – be their own masters – invent some sort of happiness for themselves outside God, apart from God. And out of that hopeless attempt has come...the long terrible story of man trying to find something other than God which will make him happy."
C.S. Lewis, Mere Christianity.

So perhaps we should not be so enamored with the great advances of technology. There is too much temptation to think we are catching up to God, that our minds and our abilities can rival His. The last thing most of us want to hear is, "Don't make me come down there!"

Let's not be so concerned about making a name for ourselves. Instead let's spend our time and energy praising His name. That's the name that really matters. All power and glory to God, now and forever!

25.

SEASONS

Winter seems to be having a hard time saying goodbye this year. Winter is like a person trying to get the last word in on an argument. It keeps coming back through the door and saying, "And for another thing!"

As I write this, I am in Indianapolis watching the snow blow and dance outside my window. It really is beautiful to watch. I live in South Carolina where snow is more or less a novelty. But here I am, still appreciating it in April. Yes, I did say snow and April in the same sentence.

The other day, I was admiring the beautiful tulips beginning to bloom in my son's front yard here in Indiana. Today they are shivering and wearing a blanket of white. Seasons can be fickle that way. Even though my calendar says spring, Mother Nature seems to want the last word in this annual conflict.

We have often heard our lives referred to in the form of seasons. Childhood, parenthood, middle age and old age have been compared to the four seasons, spring, summer, fall and winter. Each stage has its own beauty and conflict. Each season has a beginning and an end. Sometimes it is clear where one season begins and another ends. Most of the time the transition is gradual and there are no clear lines of demarcation.

The obvious bookends of our human lives are birth and death. The seasons of our lives bring a series of continual changes that we normally see clearly only in hindsight. These changes are the physical seasons in life.

We have another set of seasons in our lives. These are spiritual seasons. While the changes in the physical seasons can be hard to see and understand, changes in our spiritual seasons can be even harder to grasp. We often have trouble understanding what season we are in at any given time.

When we first become believers in Christ, we are baby Christians. We have limited knowledge and experience living a faith filled life. As we feed ourselves on the word of God we begin to grow as believers. We learn how to walk upright in faith. Our trust in God becomes stronger and the tree of our faith begins to take root and becomes tall and shady. As we grow in our faith it is important that we communicate with God. The time we spend in study, prayer and silence strengthens our relationship, faith, trust and understanding of God.

Our physical age has no bearing on our spiritual age. Physically I am in the fall of my life. My husband just retired, my youngest just turned 22 and I am experiencing the joy of being a grandmother. I don't think that I have reached that season in my spiritual life yet. I have so much to learn and so far to go. I pray I will continue to grow and mature in my spiritual life so long as I am breathing.

How about you? Do you know your spiritual season?

A good test of where we are in our spiritual growth is how we handle the inevitable challenges of life. Hard times come and go. The trials of life come and go. Where we turn for guidance determines the outcome of every trial we face. We will stumble and we will fall as we find our legs in the Christian life. We will be able to stand again after a fall if we take His hand. We can finish the race of life if we hang on tight and don't let go. We can walk hand in hand with God all the way through the gates of heaven.

God determines our seasons in life. He has His own plan for the various times of our lives.

It is not for you to know times or seasons that the Father has fixed by his own authority. (Acts 1:7 ESV)

It's our job to place our hand in His and enjoy the stroll through the seasons of our lives.

26.

THE POWER OF GOD

Every day when I sit down to write, I begin with prayer. I ask God to guide my mind. I ask Him to use me as a vessel for His own ends. I pray that He gives me the power and ability to write the things that He wants me to communicate to the world. I trust that He will show me the way and then I begin to work.

Lately when I have said these prayers, a phrase has been at the forefront of my mind. Four words have been repeating themselves over and over in my thoughts. Those four words were: "The Power of God."

There are times in all our lives when we feel powerless over a situation. We are overwhelmed and hopeless. We fear things will never change. Or perhaps worse, it could be that major changes are taking place in our lives that we don't like. We wrestle with problems that seem impossible to solve. We can't see how any good resolution could ever be possible.

We may think that such a situation could never bring any good to our lives. We certainly don't see the situation as a blessing from God. Just the opposite, it seems like a curse or a punishment.

At these times we may be selling God short. Our God is a God of impossibilities, and a God of unending miracles. No situation is out of His control. No situation is so terrible that

He cannot make it work for our spiritual benefit. And in so doing, the entire matter works to the glory of God.

Moses felt overwhelmed when God told him to go to Pharaoh with his demand to "Let my people go!" What an impossible task for someone with a speech impediment! How could he plead God's case before the Pharaoh with such limitations? Who would ever take such a man seriously?

Gideon had major self-esteem issues. He was stunned when an angel appeared to him on the threshing floor. The angel told Gideon, "Go with all your strength and save Israel from the Midianites. I am sending you to do it." I am sure he wondered, "Who, me?"

Both of them must have been in shock. But ultimately, they trusted God and did as they were told. God worked awesome miracles through these men. Through their faith they allowed God to use them for His glory. God has always been faithful to those who put their full trust in Him. God goes ahead of us and prepares the way.

Nehemiah was a cupbearer to the King of Persia. Nehemiah heard that a small remnant of Jews back in Judea was suffering. The latest news from back home was that walls of Jerusalem were breaking down. Nehemiah asked the King for permission to go back to Jerusalem to rebuild the walls. To his surprise, the King not only granted him permission, he even gave Nehemiah the timber he would need for the job from the King's own private forest.

There is no way Nehemiah could have seen how this would turn out. He barely had the courage to bring up the matter to the King in the first place. He went to God first for the answers. He must have prayed some very big prayers. God gave him the courage to approach the King, and his impossible situation had a wonderful resolution.

God wants us to pray large prayers. He wants us to pray specifically for what we need. He is a large God, a God of details. The answers we get will often astound us. But first we have to ask for His help.

Ask, and it will be given to you; seek, and you will find; knock, and the door will be opened to you. For everyone who asks receives; the one who seeks finds; and to the one who knocks, the door will be opened. (Matthew 7:7-8)

The power of God is limitless. If He can create the universe out of nothing, surely He can help us overcome our small burdens. Our problems may seem like mountains to us, but the One who created the mountains will carry us to the top and beyond.

Mary Slessor was a missionary who served in Africa. Her friends were amazed at the way she seemed able to get whatever she needed for her work from the leaders of the tribes she visited. She was said to "mold savage chiefs to her will." After her death, the tribal leaders were asked what power this humble woman possessed. One of them replied, "You have evidently forgotten to take into account the size of this woman's God."

Mary Slessor's God is the same God we pray to every day. He is the same God that worked through Moses, Gideon and Nehemiah for the benefit of those they led. He is the same God who works in the lives of all His believers.

Your prayers are just as precious to God as those forlorn prayers we read about in the Old Testament. Place your burden, whatever it is, in the hands of the Lord. He is waiting for you to ask. He wants you to know and experience His truth and his power.

Every good and perfect gift is from above, coming down from the Father of the heavenly lights, who does not change like shifting shadows. (James 1:17)

Place your problems in His capable hands and let His power move in your life. Let Him deal with whatever situation is causing your heavy heart and your restless mind. No matter how hard your situation appears, when you come to God, you've come to the right place.

27.

THE FAITH OF A CHILD

Have you ever seen a child delight in their love of Jesus? It is so simple, so joyous and so pure that it causes me to be jealous of their complete love and acceptance of Him. They never question. They just trust and believe.

Jesus said, "Truly I tell you, unless you change and become like little children, you will never enter the kingdom of heaven." (Matthew 18:2) I believe what Jesus was referring to was childlike trust, love, and faith.

When I think of a child delighting in faith of our Lord, I picture a small exuberant child, three or four years old. She is running toward her parents with a picture in her tiny hand. In her innocence and joy she is anxious to show the work of her heart to her parents. She sings, "Mommy, Daddy, look at the picture I colored for Jesus!"

She is eager to please Jesus and gives freely of herself. She has no thoughts of theology or philosophy. She has not yet become jaded and analytical. She takes on faith what she is taught about God. She feels the truth of God in her soul. She has a simple, pure faith. She loves God with all her heart and believes the Bible stories she hears in Sunday School.

We tend to complicate things the older we get. That is exactly why God tells us to return to our childlike faith.

The second book of Kings tells us about a little girl whose faith did wonders. She was a servant girl who served the wife of Naaman, a captain in the Syrian army. Naaman was a great soldier, but he had leprosy. There was no known cure.

The servant girl was a native of Israel who had been captured by a Syrian raiding party. She was basically a slave. We don't know her name. Her name doesn't appear to be important. What was important was her faith.

One day she declared in faith to her mistress, "If only my master would see the prophet who is in Samaria! He would cure him of his leprosy."

Because of her faith, the pagan Naaman traveled to Israel seeking to restore his health. He visited the prophet Elisha. His leprosy was cured.

Because of the brave girl with bold faith, Naaman declared, "Now I know that there is no God in all the earth, but in Israel."

Naaman's healing, and the power of this little girl's faith, inspired many over the years. Centuries later it was remembered and mentioned by Jesus in the book of Luke.

Childlike faith speaks volumes. It has a pure sweetness in its innocence.

May we all be granted the gift of freedom and simple love that children find so easily. May we have a heart full of love that is simple and uncomplicated. May we allow ourselves to feel once again the exuberant faith of childhood.

We can grow up when we are older.

28.

DEGREES OF COMMITMENT

Most of us are familiar with making commitments. In fact, all of us have made various kinds of commitments in our lives. We have made commitments to our faith, our families and our jobs. We may also have made various commitments to our churches, our clubs, and our friends.

I am sure you have noticed that we have varying degrees of commitment. Our hearts are sensitive to many factors that cause us to assign different weights to different promises. What are some of these factors?

One factor will be the nature of the person to whom we make the commitment. Another will be the potential cost to us of keeping or failing to keep a particular promise. Sometimes it has to do with who is watching us as we carry out the commitment. Another factor can be what we will get in return for carrying out a commitment. In other words, "What's in it for us?" A solemn promise to a family member usually carries a different weight with us than a casual one made to a friend. Many times, the strength of our commitment varies according to the incentive that is offered to us in exchange.

If I were to put a board down on the floor and ask you to walk across it, and you do, that's not much of a commitment. What if the same board is spanning the gap between two skyscrapers? That's a lot more of a commitment because the potential cost is so great. Now, let's add another factor. The reward for crossing the board between the skyscrapers is a million dollars. The risk is still very high, but now there is a substantial reward involved. There is an incentive. Still, a person may refuse the challenge because they believe the risk of death involved is more important than any amount of money.

How about another scenario? Take the same board across the same two skyscrapers, but now your small child is alone on the other roof. He is in danger of falling off and no one is there to stop him. Your degree of commitment to this task is going to be very high. Not only would you definitely follow through, my guess is no one could talk you out of doing it.

How firm are your commitments? It is easy to stay committed in situations that don't take much effort or risk. But turn up the heat and the strength of the commitment begins to be tested. Crossing the board on the ground was easy. You would be willing to do it blindfolded. There needs to be no degree of effort because it's not much of a challenge.

Crossing the board between the skyscrapers for the monetary reward is different. There is a risk but there is also a serious reward. It's optional.

When your child is on the other side of the chasm, things are once again very different. You don't have a lot of options here. If you don't cross over, your child will die. Failure to carry through means loss of life to your child, a tragedy that would forever change your life and the lives of many other people. You have no good option but to cross that board and save your child. You are their only hope. That wooden plank becomes a bridge between life and death. Now you are fully and completely committed.

Notice that in these last two cases, once the challenge is accepted, everything else fades from importance. The task at hand is "do or die."

Jesus faced a similar situation. The wooden plank for him was in the form of a cross. The chasm it divided was between heaven and hell. Out of a love that is even greater than a parent's love, Jesus gave his life to rescue us as God's children so that we could have eternal life. That was the ultimate commitment. The stakes were high, but his involvement was deep.

A couple of weeks ago I attended a seminar for Christian writers. It was held at The Cove, Billy Graham's teaching and training center in Asheville, North Carolina. After one of the sessions, I stopped in the bookstore. I came across a wonderful book called "Twelve Extraordinary Women," by John MacArthur. As I browsed through the table of contents, my eyes noticed the name of one of my favorite women in the Bible.

There was also a prophet, Anna, the daughter of Penuel, of the tribe of Asher. She was very old; she had lived with her husband seven years after her marriage, and then was a widow until she was eighty-four. She never left the temple but worshiped night and day, fasting and praying. (Luke 1:36-37)

Anna was a Jewish prophetess. The term "prophetess" meant that she was a woman who spoke the Word of God. Anna most likely taught the Old Testament to other women. She knew the Old Testament inside and out. Anna was a faithful believer in Israel. She was part of the Jewish remnant. More importantly, she was waiting patiently for the Messiah.

Anna knew from her reading of prophecy in the Old Testament, that the time for the birth of Messiah was drawing near.

At the time of this story, Anna was approaching the end of her life. She lived in the Temple and had done so for a long time. She likely lived in a small room on the temple grounds, just off the outer courts. She served the Lord with fasting and prayers. Anna talked to everyone she met about the coming Messiah. She prayed to be able to see Him before she died.

God honored Anna by answering her prayer. It happened on the day Mary and Joseph brought Jesus to the Temple to be blessed. Just as Simeon was blessing the young boy, Anna walked by and suddenly stopped. At long last she saw what she had been waiting for all her life - the Messiah.

Coming up to them at that very moment, she gave thanks to God and spoke about the child to all who were looking forward to the redemption of Jerusalem. (Luke 2:38)

This woman of great faith and constant prayer lived her entire life fully committed. Her commitment was driven by a great desire to see Jesus in the flesh. God honored her commitment with a great blessing. She was one of the first people to see the Christ and know exactly who He was.

The power of commitment in Anna's heart was given to her as a gift of the Holy Spirit. This very same gift is in the heart of every believer of Christ. Anna was faithful and diligent in her commitment to the Messiah. Her story reminds us to do the same.

Anna was an extraordinary woman. We are called upon by her example to closely examine our faith. We are called upon to examine just how far we are willing to go to share our faith and the message of the Messiah.

May we all share the same blessing as Anna and be privileged to one day gaze upon the face of Jesus in Heaven. God is "able to do immeasurably more than all we ask or

imagine, according to His power that is at work within us."
(Ephesians 3:20)

29.

TALE OF TWO WOLVES

One evening an old Cherokee Indian chief told his grandson about a battle that goes on inside every person. He said, "My son, there is a battle between two wolves that live inside of each one of us. One wolf is Evil. It is anger, envy, jealousy, sorrow, regret, greed, arrogance, self-pity, guilt, resentment, inferiority, lies, false pride, superiority, and ego.

The other wolf is Good. It is joy, peace, love, hope, serenity, humility, kindness, benevolence, empathy, generosity, truth, compassion and faith."

The grandson considered it all for a few minutes and then asked his grandfather, "Which wolf will win?"

The old Cherokee simply replied, "The one you feed."

I hope you see the truth in this old Indian tale. This is one of those little bits of wisdom that smacks me right between the eyes. I love simple, straight forward stories that force me to examine my life and lead me to contemplate adjustments that may need to be made.

So, I have to ask myself: Which wolf do I feed? At times I feed both. This is true for most of us. But which wolf do I feed the most? Which one is heavier, stronger, more in control? Which wolf's growl is the loudest in my mind?

I have to decide every morning which wolf to feed. I can feed my soul with joy and love, or I can give my soul a steady diet of pride, anger, and self-centeredness. The mind is powerful. It has the ability to heal and it also has the power to make us sick.

Our minds were the first computers. They invented "garbage in – garbage out" long before Silicon Valley. They give us the power to create and the power to kill. They give us the information that we need to build up or to tear down. They control every thought that leads us to action and every word that falls from our mouths.

There is nothing more important, useful or dangerous to man than his own mind. That's why positive thoughts and actions are so important. They define who we are and what we do as followers of God. We need the positive strength that prayer gives us every day as we go through the battles of life.

The Apostle Paul comes to mind whenever I consider how evil and good can work in a person's life. Paul spent the first part of his life persecuting Christians. He was full of hate for Christ and His followers. He had nothing but evil intentions towards them.

After his conversion, he became a powerful force for good. He considered it his privilege to suffer for Christ. His thinking was completely turned around. His thoughts in turn affected his emotions and actions. Paul was a positive influence in the life of every person he met. It is an amazing story.

The really amazing thing is this – we can do the same thing! We can change our thinking through Christ. We can inspire others. We can spread love and joy to the people we interact with every day.

This is a prayer that I wrote for myself to help me become a more positive person. I want to share it here to support others who have a similar struggle in their lives.

Dear Heavenly Father. Please feed my soul today. Guide my thoughts so they will bring happiness, beauty and joy to all I encounter today, as well as to myself. Help my eyes focus on those in need around me. Let my actions of support be selfless and abundant. Please allow my heart to overflow with the same unconditional love for others that you extend to me. Help me be a positive influence within my community. Let me spread the seeds of hope that will feed others today and every day. Guide my feet to share your truth and teach my arms to embrace those standing near me. Help me be fully present in your love and grace. Amen.

30.

RIGHT VS. WRONG

This is a call for Christian leaders to come out and take a stand for the truth. We are living in turbulent times. The country is divided and is becoming more so every day.

Where are our Christian leaders? Why are they so afraid to step forward and speak the truth? Regardless of the cost, we Christians are called to speak out against hate and injustice. Jesus did! He was all about His Father's business. He was a man on a mission. His mission was changing lives and saving souls. Shouldn't every believer have the same mission? The time has come. The moment is now. Forget the speaking engagements. Forget your book sales. Forget the number of followers on your social media accounts. Use your voice and your influence to call for truth and justice in our country.

Rest assured that I am not a devotee of any political party. I try to cast my vote for the best person for the job regardless of their label. I look for the person who represents what I stand for, for what aligns with my moral standards, my beliefs and my social conscience. With that said, I have a few questions to ask to anyone who happens to be listening and who is searching for the truth also.

When did right become wrong and wrong become right?

The truth is the truth and a lie is a lie. There is no point in calling a lie an "alternative fact." When did we become a society of delicate flowers? Our pioneer forefathers wouldn't have made it across the first wide stream on their way out West if they were as tender as we have become. Has the term "politically incorrect" become a code word for "alternative realities" like "alternative facts?" We don't need more lies, we need more truth!

When did "alternative facts" become acceptable? An "alternative fact" is nothing but a lie. Plain and simple, it is a lie. No matter who says it, it is a lie. You can color it any way you want, but it is still a lie.

We have all told lies at some point in our lives. Most of us learned how to lie as children. We thought that if we offered "alternative facts" supporting some transgression it might save us from getting in trouble. Actually, most of us found that it was the lying that got us in the most trouble.

As we matured, we grew to understand that lying was morally wrong. Honestly, we may have felt tempted at times, but as our moral fiber became stronger, so did our ability to stand up and tell the truth. Honesty became important to us as Christians. Honesty is a positive character quality.

They all fool and defraud each other; no one tells the truth. With practiced tongues they tell lies; they wear themselves out with all their sinning. (Jeremiah 9:5 NLT)

Watching the news wears me out! The media appears to have chosen sides, right and left. So where is the truth? I imagine that it is somewhere in the middle. What has happened to the days of news we could accept with confidence, spoken in the factual style of Walter Cronkite?

I find it disturbing when the leaders of our country do not speak the truth. Why do those around them look the other way? Why are they not held accountable? We have to take a stand for what scripture teaches us. If we Christians let it all slide we are nothing but lukewarm believers at best. Jesus hated lukewarm believers.

So, because you are lukewarm, neither hot or cold, I will spit you out of my mouth. (Revelation 3:16 ESV)

What disturbs me even more are the people who should know better. There are elements of the Christian faith who accept lies and immorality in our government in order to advance their own standing. Just because someone calls themselves a Christian doesn't make it so. Sometimes it just means they want to sugar coat an earthly agenda.

Beware of false prophets, who come to you in sheep's clothing, but inwardly are ravenous wolves. (Matthew 7:15 ESV)

Jesus spoke against hypocrisy. The Pharisees and Sadducees frustrated Jesus because they had double standards and "fake" ways. They elevated themselves above others in their community, but they themselves were unable to see the truth. Jesus was standing right there in front of them and they were too blind to see His significance.

What would we do if Jesus was here in front of us today? Would we be able to see and accept Him for who and what He truly is? Would there be repentance? Or would we write Him off as a long haired radical liberal and refuse to listen?

Woe to you teachers of the law. (Matthew 23:13)

So how can we tell if someone is really a Christian? We can start by looking at their actions. If a person is a true Christian, their lives will display the fruits of the spirit. If their tree is full of good fruit, that's a good sign. But if you see only poisonous, rotten fruit, you have to assume otherwise.

A good tree produces good fruit, and a bad tree produces bad fruit. A good tree cannot produce bad fruit and a bad tree cannot produce good fruit. (Matthew 7: 17-18 NLT)

What are the fruits of the Holy Spirit? The fruits of the Spirit are generosity, modesty, patience, love, self-control, faithfulness, joy, goodness, gentleness, peace, kindness and chastity. Read that list again. Use it as a checklist to assess those who claim to be sent from God to lead and guide us. If there are big red "X" marks through each item on the list, then perhaps we should look for better leaders.

When one becomes a believer, they begin to shed their old ways. Change begins on the inside. The heart grows softer and bigger. The crust of the hardness in their soul begins to crumble and fall away. Life begins to look different. A sense of morality begins to take root.

Look for these attributes in other believers. It is incredible to watch the changes that take place when a person is filled with the Holy Spirit. Don't listen to what people say, watch what they do. Their actions and behaviors are far more telling. We should be careful about who we side with. When you call yourself a Christian, people are watching. Everything you say and do is scrutinized. That is as it should be.

When you call yourself a Christian, but your actions say just the opposite, you send a message to the world. The message is that Christianity is a failure, that people seeking the truth need something other than God, and that people of sincerity and integrity do not have a safe refuge in Jesus. Do I have to say that this is not the work of a true Christian? Isn't that obvious? You'd think so.

We were given the Scriptures so we would know right from wrong and good from evil. The Lord has given us a rule book. The scriptures tell us everything we need to know. They are a guide to a wholesome life in Christ. That is why we must learn and study the Word.

It takes courage to live through suffering, and it takes honesty to observe it. Not everybody is going to be honest about who and what they are. But we need to be honest with ourselves above all else. If we don't like what we find after an honest examination of our hearts and actions, we should do something about it. It may be time to dig a little deeper into scripture and begin being honest with God. Believe me, He will be honest with us. Let's commit ourselves to this good work. Let's take a stand. Let's hold ourselves and those we follow accountable.

Above all, let's do it all with unflinching honesty.

We move toward maturity when we honestly accept who we are, understand what we can do, accept both, and live for God's glory. – Warren Wiersbe

31.

BETTER TO GIVE THAN RECEIVE

It is not what we are given in life, it's what we do with what we are given. This idea is a useful way of judging who and what we are. It can also help us figure out where we can best use our gifts and talents going forward. We can use it to set our priorities in life. We can use it as a principle of refinement and growth.

We all have known incredibly talented people. They seem to be everywhere. We read about them. We see them in sports and in the media. Their talents make them stand out from the crowd.

Most of us wish we had that kind of talent. It seems so easy for some people even as we resign ourselves to the ranks of the ordinary. However, we have all been given unique and special talents and gifts. We just need to let God use our talents in the ways that He wants us to.

Is there a difference between a talent and a gift? I think so. I see a talent as a blessing from God. It is a special ability that God gave us at birth. It is a physical or mental ability that lets us do something better than most people.

On the other hand, a gift is the result of how we use our talents. A true gift enables us to use our talents to make other lives better. It is the inclination and effort to use that talent in a beneficial way that makes the difference.

The wise use of our gifts can improve life on earth and beyond. A gift may increase our own quality of life, but a real gift benefits everyone around us. When we use our gifts properly, we increase our own sense of fulfillment and happiness. It makes us feel good to do good for others.

The cultivation of a talent into a gift is hard work but very fulfilling and very rewarding. There are thousands upon thousands of people who have done this hard work. Many such people receive little or no attention. Many people who do the greatest good for mankind receive little worldly recognition. We all know truly incredible people who do tremendous work in our world. Such people are rarely rich and famous. They may not be recognized at all beyond their immediate community.

If one is using their gifts for the glory of God, recognition is not necessary. Selfish glory is unrewarded glory in the end. Everything depends on the motivation behind our actions. A true gift serves others and is a motive unto itself. If we seek to serve ourselves at the expense of others, we have it exactly backwards.

Let's take a deeper look at the spiritual gifts that can be shared with others. We all have talents, and we have the ability and potential to develop these talents into gifts of the spirit. The seven gifts of the Holy Spirit are often listed as wisdom, understanding, counsel, fortitude, knowledge, piety, and fear of the Lord.

Our talents become spiritual gifts from God only through hard work and dedication. Our talents and the resulting gifts are as unique as we are.

With God's guidance, our individual personalities shape our talents towards service. The result is a sense that this is what we were created to do. We have the feeling that our actions serve to further the Kingdom of God here on earth and thereafter. This is a reward that no Academy Award could compete with. The development and proper use of our talents and gifts may be the very reason for our existence.

As each has received a gift, use it to serve one another as good stewards of God's varied grace; whoever speaks, as one who speaks oracles of God; whoever serves, as one who serves by the strength that God supplies – in order that in everything God may be glorified through Jesus Christ. To him belong glory and dominion forever and ever. Amen. (1 Peter 4:10-11 ESV)

Before my husband retired, we lived in a busy coastal town in South Carolina. I was very active in my church. I was in charge of the women's ministry there. I love setting up Bible Studies and I love developing various programs and seminars for women.

I also participated in a missionary team that traveled to India regularly. I went there four times. Some of the most incredible times in my life were on my journeys in India.

When we moved to the upstate of South Carolina, I had to leave a lot of that behind me. It took a couple of years before I could find a community of women that were going in the same direction that I was.

In the meantime, the character of my service to God had to change. I prayed constantly. I have always loved writing, but I always found myself too busy to sit long enough to organize my thoughts. Now I had the time I needed to be reflective. I felt the opportunity to love and serve the Lord by being alone at my keyboard.

I pray daily asking God to take whatever writing talent I may have and transform it into a gift for others. You are reading the results of those prayers. I also pray to find new avenues of service. I have joined a women's Bible study in a nearby town and that may be the avenue for yet another kind of service. I am confident that whatever God's plan for my future is, He will put my feet on that path.

If we are unsure of what our talents are, let us ask God in prayer. He will provide the answer. He will make it known. He will give us the opportunity to use our talents as gifts to others. All we have to do is be willing. When God calls us, He will equip us. Our obedience in this way will take us places we never dreamed of and our accomplishments will be pleasing to God. What more could we want out of life?

From everyone who has been given much, much will be demanded; and from the one who has been entrusted with much, much more will be asked. (Luke 12:48)

Someday I will have to stand before God and account for myself. I'm sure I'll have some big explaining to do. The most important line of questioning may involve the issue of what I did with what I was given here on earth. Did I recognize my talents? Did I turn my talents over to God? Was I a servant to my brothers and sisters? Did I turn my talents into a gift to God? If I have done all that I could, perhaps I will hear the sweetest words of all.

"Well done, good and faithful servant."

Pray and search your heart for the talents you were born with. Work with God to turn your talents into gifts of service for others. There may be fame and fortune to be had. It is far more likely that you will toil in obscurity but be rich beyond your wildest dreams with spiritual blessings and a sense of personal satisfaction.

You will see God in the eyes of those you serve. And when your time on earth is done, perhaps you will be rewarded with the greatest prize any person could ever seek. Perhaps God will say to you, "Well done, my good and faithful servant."

32.

A BLANKET OF GRACE

One of my favorite things in the world is to watch the snow falling. When I go to my happy place in my mind I am sitting by a large window, watching the snow fall with a large fireplace roaring next to me.

I grew up in Wisconsin. Snowstorms and winter activities were an integral part of my life. When I was twenty-seven, I moved to the warmth of South Carolina. I never thought I would miss the snow.

Then I experienced my first Christmas in the South. That year it was seventy-five degrees! With each passing year my longing for snow covered mornings grew deeper. It does snow in South Carolina, but the experience is very different. It snows infrequently, and it doesn't stay very long.

Everyone who knows me knows how much I love snow. And here is the funny part. For years after I moved south, I was known as "Snow Repellent." It never seemed to snow where I was. It could be snowing all over the whole state, but it would miss our town. When we traveled outside South Carolina, that is the time it would snow at our house.

When we went north to places where it snowed all the time, it would snow there the week before, and it would snow the week after. It never snowed while I was there. If my husband or kids took a trip, they would get the snow. I stayed home and got a cold drizzle or blue skies.

When my husband retired, we moved to the foothills of the mountains in South Carolina. The curse of being "Snow Repellent" has at long last been lifted and now I am blessed to spend several happy days each winter watching the snowflakes fall.

You may be asking, "What's the attraction?" Maybe you live in an area that is overloaded with snow every year. In that case you might not share my appreciation. Or maybe you are a fan of warm weather like my husband, who shivers any time the temperature drops below 40. Let me tell you why I find snow so enchanting.

Snow truly is magical to me. I love the downward drift of thousands upon thousands of snowflakes. I find it extremely peaceful. It calms my soul. The world is quiet and still. For a moment, I feel like I can hear myself think again. My thoughts float back to childhood and all the happy times I spent playing in that cold fluffy white stuff. I remember the sheer delight of "snow days." I even remember with great fondness being held captive indoors while the wind huffed and puffed, blowing white gusts in swirls around the corners of the house. Of course, I also remember frozen fingers and toes and eyelashes stuck together, but that was a small price to pay.

The other day I awoke to a snow-covered countryside here in the mountains. As my husband and I drove into town, I marveled at the blanket of white that covered the entire ground. I thought about the grace of God. It covers our sins, just like the blanket of snow that morning covered the landscape. Under the snow was the earth. It was full of life laid dormant, seeds and flowers waiting to be born, bulbs waiting to burst forth, and trees waiting to put forth new leaves. The earth will return to life when the promise of spring is fulfilled. The stillness of a winter's day is a time of waiting, peacefully and beautifully, for the world to once again become busy and full of new things.

The flowers and trees will bloom and become fragrant. The grass will go from brown to green and the air will turn warm. The earth will be renewed.

The grace of God covers believers in Jesus just like that blanket of snow. When we become calm and still in prayer, we can see the beauty of the world. We were dormant, devoid of color and fragrance, but our faith in the Son brings our lives into full bloom.

One day all the dirt of our lives will be completely washed away. The seeds of our human souls will sprout and grow into blossoms of unimaginable glory in God's garden. The dull brown times of our life will be behind us. We will be as individual as snowflakes, and we will radiate with the love of our Heavenly Father. We will know at last who we really are meant to be in eternity.

A.W. Tozer said it this way:

Grace is the good pleasure of God that inclines Him to bestow benefits upon the undeserving. It is a self-existent principle inherent in the divine nature and appears to us as a self-caused propensity to pity the wretched, spare the guilty, welcome the outcast, and bring into favor those who were before under just disapprobation. Its use to us sinful men is to save us and make us sit together in heavenly places to demonstrate to the ages the exceeding riches of God's kindness to us in Christ Jesus.

In the meantime, I say, "Let it snow!"

33.

COLOR OR CONTENT?

I sometimes attend a church in my town that ministers to the homeless. On any given Sunday, homeless people make up a large segment of the congregation. Some of the attendees have not showered in a few days. There aren't many suits and ties. Some of the people are mentally ill and can't sit still or be quiet. There are people there of every race and background. Quite a few have spent time in jail or mental hospitals. There are prostitutes and drug addicts. There are lots of people with physical ailments.

It's where Jesus would go to church if he were here today. I have no doubt about that. These are his kind of people.

The homeless are part of the church services. They serve as ushers, and they take up the collection. They read from the pulpit. There are singers and musicians who participate regularly. Sometimes those in attendance are treated to something truly unforgettable. Today was one of those days.

As I write this, it is the day before the Martin Luther King Jr. holiday. Here in the South, the holiday is a day for celebration, pride and hope, especially in the African American community.

It's a big day at this church. The pastor's sermon always focuses on social justice and how far we have come - and how far we have to go.

Today there was a special treat. An older black man took the pulpit and recited the entire "I Have A Dream" speech. He did it all from memory. It was amazing and awe inspiring. This man was old enough to remember Dr. King. He grew up with the hope that the words of Dr. King's dream could become a reality. It was important enough to him that he committed himself to learning every word of the speech.

His current address is the local Salvation Army shelter.

Dr. King believed that the silence of good people was appalling. He believed the writers of the Declaration of Independence spoke the truth when they said that all men were created equal in the sight of God. Along with them he believed that this equality gave all men the right to pursue life, liberty, and happiness. These principles are the very foundation of our nation. If Dr. King were alive today, what would he see? What would he say?

I have a feeling he would say that he still has a dream of equality, but that it's not here yet. He would still be appalled at the silence of good people in the face of evil.

Dr. King did not just speak for African Americans. He spoke on behalf of every person of every color, no matter who they were, or where they came from. He spoke for all of those who were not yet an equal part of our society.

Some things have changed, but we have a long way to go. We continue to fight the same old fight against ignorance, prejudice, and persecution. I'm sure Dr. King would still be speaking out about these issues. His dream would no doubt include immigrants and refugees in its scope were he to speak out today.

Do not forget to show hospitality to strangers, for by so doing some people have shown hospitality to angels without knowing it. (Hebrews 13:12)

The official narrative is that America has always been a melting pot. Our ancestors were welcomed with open arms and given a chance to pursue a better life in this land. They had the opportunity to make the best living they could for themselves and their families. This picture of course, is only partially true.

The hard truth is that many people were not welcomed or accepted in this country. At various times, the list included (among many others) the Irish, Armenians, African Americans, Hispanics, Muslims, Jews, Catholics, people from the Middle East, the Chinese, and of course women. Anyone who was not a member of a particular group of white males of European ancestry had an uphill fight to get ahead in American society.

Now there are those who want America to close her doors. They want to blame all the current troubles of this country on the immigrant and the refugee. Instead of being Good Samaritans, many people seem to be headed in the opposite direction. Racism and intolerance are a growing concern in our culture.

Dr. Martin Luther King Jr. spoke every chance he could against hearts and minds that housed hatred and bigotry. When I was young, I thought that the Civil Rights movement would eventually lead our country to a new birth of freedom for all its people. A lot has been accomplished but there are many miles left to go.

Jesus extended salvation to all who believed that he was the Son of God. That invitation was open to ALL people, not just men of a specific color or from certain places. God wants us all to have freedom and equality. That was how man was created, and that is how it will be one day in Heaven.

Good men do not remain silent in the face of injustice. Jesus rarely hesitated to speak out when confronted with evil.

Dr. King said, "If America is to become a great nation equality must become true." That principle is important for all kinds of people. No matter what you may have heard, this is the real way America will become great again.

As a minister, Dr. King often quoted scripture in his speeches. In his most famous speech, he took part of his text from Isaiah.

Fill in the valleys, and level the mountains and hills. Straighten the curves, and smooth out the rough places. Then the glory of the Lord will be revealed, and all people will see it together. The Lord has spoken! (Isaiah 40:4-5 NLT)

Thank you, God, for the lives of great people like Dr. King. Let us all strive to make his dream a reality in our country. Let us put aside our differences and let us work together to make equality and justice a fact instead of something we just hope for one day.

34.

BLESSINGS OF AN UNSAVORY SOUL

Words of wisdom often come from the last place you would expect. Have you ever been surprised that way? It happens to me a lot. A small child may say something wise and profound. Sometimes a person I thought had nothing important to say to me says the very thing that I needed to hear and take to heart. God moves in mysterious ways. God also moves in this way to teach me not to judge or assume things about people.

More times than I care to admit, I have received answers to my prayers from unlikely sources. It always brings me up short. It reminds me that I simply don't know very much. God seldom answers my prayers the way I imagine He should. His messages and His messengers can come from anywhere and anyone.

"For my thoughts are not your thoughts, neither are your ways my ways," declares the Lord, "As the heavens are higher than the earth, so are my ways higher than your ways and my thoughts than your thoughts. (Isaiah 55:8-9)

The Jews expected the Messiah to come as a king. When He finally came to them, very few people recognized Him as the one they had been waiting for. He didn't match their idea of what a king should look like. We frequently limit ourselves because we are unwilling to keep an open mind. We don't grasp the full picture.

For instance, we see someone living in a big house with nice cars and we assume that they are wealthy. We see another person living in modest means with a twenty-year-old car. We assume that person is not very wealthy. But appearances don't mean much. The first person may be mortgaged to the eyeballs, and the second person may have squirreled away a fortune through their thrift. We constantly see illusions and think that they are reality.

Jesus had very humble beginnings. He definitely did not live a life of privilege and wealth. He wandered the countryside with a rag-tag band of followers, without jobs and probably without very much money. He slept wherever He could. There is no mention of Him having any possessions beyond a robe and a pair of sandals.

In the famous paintings Jesus looks regal and dignified. He is dressed in clothes that are simple but clean. He is often shown with a halo of light around His head. He is tall and handsome.

Actually, I doubt if He was anything like that. If He had been, surely a lot more people would have recognized Him for who He was. They would have clearly seen Him as a very special person who deserved a great deal of respect. It seems clear from the Gospels that this was not the case. Not many people knew who He was. Many of the people around Him every day were not convinced of His true nature.

We do ourselves a terrible disservice when we judge people or ideas without a full investigation. Things are often not what they seem. We usually don't stop to look below the surface. We don't evaluate things for ourselves. We accept what we see as the truth and move on, oblivious to reality.

Human beings were created to be critical thinkers. We were given greater intelligence than animals for a reason. I believe God wants us to use our intelligence to be able to see beyond the illusions and wrong ideas that surround us. We are called to operate on a higher level, to be willing to investigate new ideas. And we are called upon to see the light of God in every person, no matter what their external conditions.

The unkempt person standing beside you may be the person God has sent to you to answer your prayers. Remember that the world expected pomp and circumstance surrounding the arrival of the Messiah. I'm sure they never expected Him to ride into Jerusalem on a donkey. They expected Him to be born in a palace, not in a trough were barnyard animals were fed.

They expected Him to be friends with rulers, dignitaries, high priests and other VIPs. They did not expect to find Him in the company of fisherman, sinners, tax collectors and prostitutes. They assumed that God would make the Messiah easy to spot. Instead, He was nothing like they expected Him to be.

Why did God do it this way? We might never know the real reason, but I can make a couple of guesses. For one thing, it was necessary for His followers to have a special sort of faith. If the Messiah had been easy to spot, what would have been the role of faith?

Another reason may be that God wanted to drive home to mankind how easy it is not to see the truth, even when it is standing right in front of us. When we realize how many of life's fish hooks are baited with what we think are good things, we can understand why seeing the truth is a necessary skill.

I also think that God wants us to look for the holy in every person, regardless of their outward circumstances. He wants to teach us that we have no idea how He is going to answer our prayers or who He will use to carry out His plans.

Many are the plans in a person's heart, but it is the Lord's purpose that prevails. (Proverbs 19:21)

Our preconceived ideas can cause us to overlook blessings that are right in front of us. The person we would prefer to look right past may be there to open our eyes to great things we would have otherwise missed completely.

To open our minds, we need to open our eyes and ears. We need to be patient. We need to be still and listen to what God has to say. In this way we can wipe our slate of preconceived ideas clean. We can look at the world with a clear mind, like the mind of a small child who sees things for the first time. We can see things without the burden of judgment prior to investigation.

Truly I tell you, unless you change and become like little children, you will never enter the kingdom of heaven. (Matthew 18:3)

Things are not always what they appear to be. We create our own illusions and realities in our minds. Our truths and our expectations are colored by what we believe and by what the world believes. We are wrong a lot of the time.

Mother Teresa said, "If you judge people, you have not time to love them."

I think God wants us to open our minds, hearts, ears, eyes and arms to new possibilities. We may discover that the unsavory looking soul standing in our path is an angel sent to guide us on the stony path of life. They may be here to soothe, comfort and care for us along the way.

God wants us to regularly re-examine the ideas that define our lives. He wants us to keep an open mind and an open heart. Does this sound like a radical idea? Yes, it does. Yet this is exactly what we are called upon to do.

Do not conform to the pattern of this world but be transformed by the renewing of your mind. Then you will be able to test and approve what God's will is—his good, pleasing and perfect will. (Romans 12:2)

We lived all our lives following the patterns of the world. It did not get us very far. Now we are given the opportunity to renew our minds in Christ. How can we turn down a great opportunity like that?

35.

GRACE THROUGH THE AGES

On a clear and breezy evening, a young Jewish peasant girl dreamily gazed out her window. She was romanticizing about her wedding day and the love of her fiancé, as only a young girl can do. She imagined herself in the handsome clothes that would adorn her young body on her wedding day. She thought of the different witty things she would say to the many guests who would attend the wedding feast.

She could clearly picture the look of pride on her father's face. She could almost feel the tear that was sure to run down her mother's cheek on that magical day. She couldn't wait to see the look on Joseph's face when he caught the first glimpse of his beautiful bride on their wedding day. Mary was lost in deep thought when a bright light appeared in her room.

The light was blinding and sudden. A voice rang out and shook Mary to her core. It appeared to be some kind of angel or heavenly being. Mary had never seen anything like this before.

She tried to shield her eyes with her shaking hands. Yet, there was a sense of peace that radiated from this being. He told her not to be afraid. She could feel in her heart he was not there to harm her. He knew her name. He told her she had won favor with God. But why? What had she ever done to earn God's favor?

The angel, whose name was Gabriel, went on to tell her she would conceive and give birth to a son and that He was to be called Jesus. The angel told her He would be great and would be called the Son of the Most High. He told her God would give Him the throne of His ancestor David, and He would reign over Jacob's descendants forever, a kingdom without end. (Luke 1:26-38)

Mary was terribly confused. She was young and naive, but her mother had carefully explained the nature of a physical relationship between a man and a woman when she first became betrothed to Joseph. She knew about the "birds and bees," but there had been nothing in her mother's talk about angels. It just hadn't been covered. She could not make sense of what the angel was telling her.

She asked the angel, "How will this be, since I am a virgin?" The angel's reply was both comforting and commanding. He told Mary,

> *"The Holy Spirit will come on you, and the power of the Most High will overshadow you. So the holy one to be born will be called the Son of God. Even Elizabeth your relative is going to have a child in her old age, and she who was said to be unable to conceive is in her sixth month. For no word from God will ever fail." (Luke 1:35-36)*

Mary felt the presence of God in her room as the angel spoke. Her very soul was soaring with the pounding of each heartbeat. Mary knew God was calling her to perform a very special task for Him. She knew that God's word was true. She felt honored and unworthy at the same time.

Her heart answered the angel before her mind had a chance to think. In blind faith, Mary answered, "I am the Lord's servant. May your words be fulfilled." As quickly as the light appeared, it suddenly disappeared, and Mary was left alone in the stillness of her room.

Mary must have been very conflicted after Gabriel had left her presence. She had been chosen by God to give birth to His son. What an unbelievable honor! Can you even imagine what that must have felt like? But, then again, there were some very real and practical problems to be faced if this news was true.

What would she tell Joseph? Would he believe her? Would he abandon her and leave her in disgrace? What would her friends and family think? Her father especially would be disgraced. He was going to be quite angry with her. Her whole family was likely to be ashamed of her.

She lived in a small community. The gossip would be endless. She and her family could become outcasts. There must have been a thousand thoughts running through Mary's mind. But her faith gave her strength. She knew that God had a plan and that it would succeed. That is where she found her courage.

She looked to heaven as she walked in faithful obedience to God. He would guide her path as she carried and cared for His Son. Through His grace, Mary became the mother of grace.

Mary had been chosen by God to be the *theotokos*. In Greek, theotokos means the Mother of God. She would be blessed among all women. She would be the Mother of the Messiah. Her son would be the Savior of the world.

As a good Jewish girl, she was familiar with scripture. The angel told her that her baby would one day inherit the throne of David. She knew that Joseph was from the direct lineage of David. Mary had always found much encouragement from the life of David.

Gazing out her window, Mary began to replay in her mind what had just occurred. Her thoughts led her to scripture and to 1 Chronicles 17:23, 24. David said to the Lord, "Let the promise you have made concerning your servant and his house be established forever. Do as you promised, so that it will be established and that your name will be great forever,"

Mary couldn't help but realize the similarities between her answer to the Lord and David's. Then Mary recalled other verses from 1 Chronicles. In 1 Chronicles 17:16, David said to the Lord, "Who am I Lord God, and what is my family, that you have brought me this far?"

Mary felt the same honor and grace that David must have felt all those years ago. Then she recalled another verse in Chronicles that she had read some time ago. In 1 Chronicles 17:17, "God looked at him (David) as though he were the most exalted of men."

Mary felt a strong bond with David and a connection with him that would remain in her heart forever. She too felt exalted among women. She marveled at the similarities between her and David. Mary knew that this baby boy that she would carry would be placed in the line of David forever.

God has offered His gift of grace to man from the beginning. We saw God's grace being offered to Abraham as the father of the Jewish nation. His grace filled the lives of Jacob, Isaac, Joseph and their descendants. King David was a part of the lineage of grace that would be brought to full fruition in Mary's womb.

Jesus extends that same grace to us. There is grace for all who believe in Him, Jews and Gentiles alike. Grace was with us in the beginning and it is with us now. That grace has a face. It is the face of Jesus Christ, the Son of the Most High God, who was born as a baby on Christmas morning. He would offer His life as a sacrificial lamb. He would rise from the dead on Easter morning. Christ would pay the ultimate price so that the free gift of grace could be obtained by all.

Let's not forget to give praise to God for counting us worthy of the gift of grace. It is the most precious gift we could ever hope for. It can never be duplicated or replaced. On the day that Christ was born, it was mankind who received the ultimate gift. Like Mary and like David, we are honored and blessed beyond measure.

May you feel the bounty of every good and wonderful blessing from above! May you feel God's grace in your life when you need it the most!

36.

WHATS IN A NAME?

D o the names Gaspar, Balthasar and Melchior mean anything to you? Until a couple of weeks ago I certainly would have said not.

But actually, we have known about these gentlemen all of our lives. We have read about them. We have sung about them. We may have even dressed up like one of them in a Christmas pageant. If you haven't guessed by now, they are the three wise men who visited the baby Jesus.

The wise men were astrologers. They studied the stars. When a new star appeared in the sky, they were naturally very interested. They were very learned men. They knew and studied holy writings from many cultures, including the Hebrew scriptures.

They would have been familiar with these words of prophecy:

But you, Bethlehem Ephrathah, though you are small among the clans of Judah, out of you will come for me one who will be ruler over Israel, whose origins are from of old, from ancient times. (Micah 5:2)

They were probably also familiar with Daniel's prophecy. Daniel had said:

I see him, but not now; I behold him, but not near. A star will come out of Jacob; a scepter will rise out of

Israel. He will crush the foreheads of Moab, the skulls of all the people of Sheth. (Numbers 24:17)

The wise men were noble men of wealth. That's why they could afford their generous gifts of gold, frankincense and myrrh. Their names are full of meaning.

The name Gaspar means "Treasure." Balthasar means "Protect the King." Melchior's name means, "King City." These three kings lived up to their names.

They brought earthly treasure as gifts to the baby Jesus. They protected Jesus by not reporting His location to Herod, who they suspected wanted this baby killed. Any city where a King is born can be called the City of the King. And here they were in Bethlehem.

It is obvious from the Bible that names were very important. They were so important that God changed peoples' names from time to time to make His meaning for their lives clear. Abram became Abraham, Simon became Peter, Saul became Paul, and Jacob became Israel.

God Himself has many names that tell us about who He is: I Am, Lord of Lords, King of Kings, King of the Jews, The Alpha and Omega, The Bread of Life, The Bridegroom, The Deliverer, The Good Shepherd, The High Priest, The Lamb of God, The Light of the World, The Messiah, The Rock, The Risen Lord, The Son of Man, The Word, The Savior, and The Truth.

These various names of God help us understand who He is. The names of the three wise men help us understand who they were and what Jesus would later do.

He Himself would become a treasure. He Himself protects us and grants us grace. And He will preside over the great City of God in Heaven.

Did you know that all of God's children will one day have a secret name?

Whoever has ears, let them hear what the Spirit says to the churches. To the one who is victorious I will give some of the hidden manna. I will also give that person a white stone with a new name written on it, known only to the one who receives it. (Revelation 2:17)

So, all of God's people have a name only known to God, a name that won't be known until the end of the age. Then we will find out what God's plan for us was, who it was He created us to be, and consequently what it was we were called to do in His service.

With this in mind, what do you think your secret name will be? Have you worked to further the kingdom of God like Abraham? Have you been a treasure to God like Gaspar? Have you repented from a life of sin like Paul? Have you been a rock of faith like Peter? Or is your secret name one that is so unique that it fits you and you alone?

I can't wait to find out my secret name, the name that describes me and which explains just what I was created to do. I ask myself, "If I died right now, this very night, what name would God reveal to me in Heaven? Would I be proud of it? Would it confirm that I have accomplished whatever it was that I was created to do? Will my name bring me honor because I lived up to it? Or will it bring me sorrow because I failed to do what I was created to do?"

If I don't like the answers, then I best get to work. It's time to seek guidance from God and get busy. I have my good name to live up to!

37.

BEGIN WITH THE WORD

I recently read a shocking statistic. Only 20% of churchgoers read the Bible regularly. That is appalling! If we Christians are supposed to be living a God centered life, where are we getting our directions from? How can we build a successful life without reading the instruction manual? I don't think we can.

The Bible is not just a guidebook. It is also a history book. We have all heard, "Those who do not learn history are doomed to repeat it." Do we really want to repeat history?

The Israelites did exactly that after Moses brought them out of Egypt. They wandered around in the desert for forty years, failing to learn what God wanted them to learn. As a result, they kept repeating the same mistakes, and they kept getting the same results.

The Bible is more than our history. It is our present and our future. It contains the answers to life's most challenging questions. It is our hope for today and the promise of tomorrow. Every book in the Bible is there to provide us with the information that we need to live as followers of God. From it we learn how to worship God, how to establish a personal relationship with Him, and how best to serve Him and our fellow man. And in it we hear the good news of salvation through Jesus Christ.

In the beginning was the Word, and the Word was with God, and the Word was God. (John 1:1)

The Word is Jesus Christ. He was present in the beginning with the Father. He is the second person in the Holy Trinity. He is omnipresent. He gave Himself as the ultimate sacrifice for the sins of man. Faith in Jesus Christ is the only way to the Father. By the grace of God, man is gifted with eternal salvation through faith in His son, Jesus Christ.

Most of us spend weeks planning our vacations but we give very little thought about where we will spend eternity. If heaven is our ultimate destination, don't we need to get precise directions on how to get there? Isn't that something we want to get right?

The Bible tells us about our origins and about the faith of our forefathers. The Bible is eternal and universal. What happened 2000 years ago is just as relevant as what is happening today.

Students of the Bible are amazed at the accuracy of the prophets. If you doubt this, I urge you to read the book of Joel. The book of Joel is as timely as the headlines in your news feed or the lead story of the nightly news. God's Word is timeless.

I grew up in a religion that did not place an emphasis on reading the Bible. In my thirties I began what has been a lifetime of catching up. With each new thing I have learned, I have fallen deeper in love with God's word.

One of my first Bible studies was about Genesis. I remember thinking that it was going to be horribly boring. I couldn't have been more wrong. As it turned out, Genesis is now one of my favorite books of the Bible.

I love discovering every nugget of Biblical truth that is placed before my heart. I hunger for God's instructions and I feast on His promises. I am comforted by the deep wisdom of the Bible. At the same time, I am challenged to courageously face my problems and shortcomings. The Bible gives me the strength and wisdom I need to deal with them. Nothing else gives me so much of what I need to successfully deal with life. Charles H. Spurgeon said,

"To me the Bible is not God, but it is God's voice, and I do not hear it without awe."

If I am not listening to God's voice, what am I listening to instead? That's a question I regularly ask myself. If I am not looking for answers in the right place, I try to change course. The right course always seems to lead me right back to the Word of God.

My prayer for you is that you will search your heart to determine whether you are listening to God's voice or to the very loud voices of this world. I pray that you will fall in love with God's Word the same way I have. I pray that you will find untold treasure there that will bring your life into alignment with God's master plan.

God will give us all the understanding and courage we need to consistently apply His lessons in our lives. We just need to sit down and carefully read His instruction manual. With His help, we can fully apply the principles of His Word to every challenge in our lives.

When all else fails, read the directions!

38.

MIRACULOUS JOY

God is never more real to us than when He answers our prayers. It is a spiritually euphoric experience.

Matthew 19:26 tells us that "With man this is impossible, but with God all things are possible." But what is the "this" that is so impossible? In the context of this verse, Jesus was talking about how hard it would be for a rich man to enter heaven. He told us that it would be easier for a camel to go through the eye of a needle.

In our lives "this" can be anything and everything. "This" is usually something that is out of our control, something that we don't have any power over, something that as mere mortals we are helpless over. If you stop and think about it, "this" can be just about anything.

We like to think that we are in control of most things in our life, but really, we are not in control of very much. We have no control over life or death. We can't control aging or illness. We have no control over what is in another person's heart and how they may react or behave as a result. We don't have control over the weather or traffic or how people around us behave. How do we get a handle on a world seemingly out of control? A couple of things are sure to help.

First, we need to remind ourselves that everything in our lives has happened for a reason. God has a plan and a purpose, and He will carry it through. Of course, many times His plan and purpose are a complete mystery to us.

We can't see how any good can ever come out of a troublesome situation. It seems impossible, it seems hopeless no matter how we look at it. At these times it is easy to feel discouraged, heartbroken and abandoned.

Second, we can be confident that God has not abandoned us, and He never will. He wants us to come to Him on a daily basis and talk with Him about our burdens and how they affect our lives. He wants to hear the pleas of our heart. He wants to hold our hands and dry our tears as we navigate the twists and turns and heartbreaks of life. He knows being a human being is hard. He knows some days we struggle just to get out of bed.

But God is faithful, and He will answer every prayer and petition we share with Him. His answers will come in His way and in His time. The most important thing that we can do is keep the daily communication going, no matter how long it may take. It can take years sometimes, but the waiting is what makes the joy of answered prayer so sweet.

J. Hudson Taylor once said,

"There are three stages in every great work of God: first, it is impossible, then it is difficult, then it is done."

I absolutely agree. That has been my exact experience. I go from "This is unfixable!" to "I guess there could be a way for things to work out, but I can't see how." Then one day, if I am faithful, I find out the answer. I get to experience the miracle of, "It is done."

Several years ago, something bad was happening in my life. It was something I had absolutely no control over. I felt like my life was in a downward spiral. The only thing that gave me hope was my faith that God was in control. I had faith that He had a plan and a purpose for me, and this helped me get to the other side of one of the darkest times of my life.

[I am] confident that God, who began this good work in you, will carry it through to completion until the day of Christ Jesus. (Philippians 1:6)

I hung onto those words. More accurately, I clung to these words with white knuckles. Some days I was flat on my face before the Lord in desperate prayer.

I didn't just pray daily. Some days my heart was so heavy that I spent the whole day in continuous silent prayer. In my mind I was standing in front of God's front door, ringing the doorbell over and over and it seemed I was getting no response. I was sure God was sick of hearing me ask Him about the same thing over and over.

But there is great news. Thank goodness He never tires of hearing heartfelt prayers from His children. After years of unceasing prayer, God finally answered my prayers. The solution He came up with was better than anything I could have imagined.

My problem went from impossible, to difficult, to God saying, "I have heard you sweet child, it is done!" There is nothing like being on the receiving end of a miracle. It is as close as we can get to heaven on earth.

What stage are you are at with the biggest and messiest problem in your life? Wherever you are, don't give up! We can't navigate our own stormy seas with any degree of certainty, so doesn't it make sense to talk daily to the One who can?

Don't get discouraged. Be patient and keep telling God your problem. Confess that you see no way it can be resolved. Admit that you have come to the end of your wits. Tell him you are putting the whole frustrating mess in His hands. Be willing to do your part, but leave the worrying to God.

The joy of answered prayer is worth the work. Go ahead and spend some serious time on your knees. Constant contact with God is the bond that connects your life to Christ. It's the joy of His heart to give you the desires of your heart.

The solution God provides may surprise you. It may be like nothing you ever imagined. His way of working it out could be a thousand times better than the outcome you hoped for.

Take your problems straight to Him and abide in faith. Miraculous joy can be yours.

39.

RAINBOWS

It's funny how everyday events can spark a truth from God's word.

I was reading the Bible story of Joseph and his coat of many colors with my grandson the other day and my mind made a delightful connection.

It struck me that the colors in Joseph's coat represent the different colors of people from the different nations that will stand before the Lord one day. Then I was reminded of two promises that God has made to mankind.

After the flood, God made a covenant with Noah and his descendants that assured them He would never again destroy the earth by flood. He placed a rainbow in the clouds as a symbol of His everlasting covenant.

God made another covenant with man. God said that all who believe in His son Jesus Christ will have eternal salvation. I love God's use of a rainbow to represent different but equal. Every color in a rainbow is there for a reason. Each color has its own specific wavelength in the light spectrum. God has placed them there as part of the makeup of visible light.

Like the colors of the rainbow, every person, no matter what their color, nation or language, is equally important to God. I am sure that Heaven will be made up of a virtual rainbow of people of all kinds. Unlike our present situation, we will not only get along with each other, we will deeply love one another. Our hearts will be freed, and we will see the glory of God within each soul.

In heaven, as here on earth, all colors in our human rainbow are important. We are all the beautiful offspring of Adam and Eve. We are all created by God for the glory of God. We are all equally precious in his eyes.

May we all be able to see the beauty in our fellow human beings. May we be able to fully share in their heartaches and their joys. Every time we see a rainbow, let's allow it to be a reminder that God loves us all equally and completely.

God created a world full of diversity. The endless variety of the world gives it richness and flavor. We honor God when we notice and appreciate that fact. Jesus knew there were differences between people, but He loved them all the same. We should aspire to do the same.

40.

WHY DO THE RIGHTEOUS SUFFER?

Was Job blessed or cursed? When someone brings up Job, the usual response is, "Oh, that poor soul. He really got a raw deal." The Job story makes me uneasy. He seems to have gotten caught up in a debate that he was not a party to.

Job was said to be blameless, but for some reason his life was destroyed. There is nothing that suggests that he deserved the hell he was put through. I find myself praying, "Oh God, please don't let anything like this ever happen to me!"

Those who have difficulty with the idea of God like to bring up this story. They squint their eyes, shake their heads and ask, "Why would God allow Satan to torture Job like that? Wasn't he a believer? Wasn't he one of God's favorites? Wasn't he a faithful man? What did he do to deserve what he got?"

Of course, those are exactly the questions that Job's story is written to discuss. The existence of evil in a world controlled by a benevolent God is a problem that has plagued thinkers for ages. It's hard to find an acceptable answer.

Job was a righteous and successful man. He had favor in God's eyes. Satan taunted God and sought permission to take away all the things Job loved. Surely then Job would curse God. God gave Satan permission to take away Job's family and possessions but told him not to harm him physically. Satan carried out his first salvo of attacks, but Job remained faithful and praised God.

Satan again challenged God. This time God allowed Satan to take Job's health but not his life. Job was covered with sores from his head to his feet and scraped at his sores with pieces of broken pottery. Job finally cried out in anguish, "Why me? What did I ever do to deserve all this?"

We can't blame Job for asking these questions. Everything he once treasured was gone. We hurt for him. His situation is heartbreaking and tragic. He was understandably hurt and confused. He thoroughly examined his life to try to figure out what he had done to lose favor with God.

Several of his friends came over to sympathize with him but they were baffled as well. There were three who assumed Job committed some secret sin and suggested that God's wrath against Job was justified. Job protested his innocence. He wanted answers, and he wanted them from God.

Another friend who was there, Elihu, weighed into the discussion. Both sides are wrong, he said. God works on an entirely different level than man. God is immeasurably greater than humans. Thus, He has plans no man can understand. God alone knows the meaning of all things, and the reasons why all things happen.

Job still was not satisfied. He continued to want answers directly from God.

God finally spoke directly to Job from out of a whirlwind. He explained nothing. He did not justify Himself. God's wisdom is His alone. He made Job understand that the complexities of God and His universe are far too deep for any man's comprehension.

Job, chastised, admitted that his limited human understanding paled before that of the Creator of the universe.

He retracted none of his questions and arguments, but he admitted the limits of his wisdom.

Ultimately God restored Job to prosperity. He gave him more wealth and prestige than ever before, and He gave him a new family to replace his loved ones who were lost.

It is easy to find problems with this story. It seems to raise more questions than it answers. Why did God give Satan permission to torment Job? Was Job wrong to complain of his treatment? Was there something in Job's past that really did justify the horrors that befell him?

The fact that Job was given a whole new family is nice enough, but how do you explain it all to Job's first family? It certainly looks like they died for no other reason than to test Job's devotion to God. The new family was not that much of a blessing to them.

The great philosophers have debated these questions for thousands of years. A truly satisfying set of answers has never been found. That troubles us because in our arrogance we believe that given enough time and effort our minds can comprehend any problem that exists.

The whole subject of divine justice is far over my head. I suspect that is the point of the book of Job. None of us want to deal with the idea that bad things can and do happen in our lives no matter what our level of devotion to God. Our belief and faith do not make us exempt from the inevitable suffering that all men must endure.

Personally, I think God allowed Satan to torment Job because He knew the depth of Job's faithfulness. God deemed Job to be the most faithful living soul on earth. Satan knows our weaknesses. He knows how to push our buttons. But he doesn't know our hearts. He doesn't know the depth of our love for God. Satan doesn't feel love. He is the opposite of love.

God, who is love, knows our hearts. He knew that Job might ask hard questions about his situation, but he would remain faithful to Him. He knew that Job might doubt God's plans (don't we all?) but He also knew Job would never abandon Him. And in the end, God did not abandon Job, but blessed him anew. Job emerged from the story with a new family, a new prosperity and with brand new possessions.

Job did not understand what was happening to him. We can identify with that. Seldom do we understand what's going on when we are caught up in the middle of one of life's storms. We wonder if God really has a purpose and a plan for our lives.

When God's plan doesn't seem to match our desires, that's not the time to give up. That's the time to stand firm in our faith and let God be in control. In such situations people often turn away from God instead of turning to God.

In this way, Job's story is a lesson to us all. Though the answers to the hardest questions of life and theology may elude us, we are still called to stay faithful and trust in His infinite wisdom. Our lack of wisdom is not an excuse for our lack of faith. We have that part exactly backwards. Our lack of wisdom is the very reason we need faith.

Whenever I study Job, I find my prayers take on a new tone. I find myself praying that God would find me to be as faithful as he found Job to be. I begin to pray that my heart would be as pure as Job's even when I have a lot of hard questions I want to ask about life.

I pray that when God's eyes search the earth, He will find my soul to be beating for Him and Him alone. My plea has changed from never wanting to be challenged, to instead asking for the strength and courage to remain faithful during every challenge in my life.

May we always stand firm in our faith! May we always hold tight to God's love and promises. When we do, we can weather any storm that blows into our lives. We can trust Him. He will never abandon us.

I no longer think of Job as having been cursed. I see him as being challenged to the depths of his soul, but in the end, he is blessed and restored by his steadfast loyalty to God.

We are all like Job. We all have heartache, loss and infirmity. We wonder why the faithful have troubles and why the wicked often seem to prosper. These questions never really leave us. But who are we to question the wisdom of our Creator? How great would He be if puny man could understand him completely?

It really does help when we can put our troubles in perspective. We all have trials and troubles that don't seem fair. But God and His wisdom endures. It encourages us to reconsider the things that we consider trials in our lives.

My prayer is that God will give us the grace to see past what we consider to be our tribulations and sorrows. We seek God's grace, serenity and wisdom. We put our trust in Him. We have faith that He has a plan. Our job is to press forward and strive to live a life of joy in the midst of troubles and suffering.

.41.

ADAM AND EVE

As I looked out my windows at the mountains this morning, I found myself in awe at the beauty of God's creation. God's handiwork was on full display. It is amazing to think he created the earth and all its beauty just to hand it over to us. The very beauty of his creation tells me that he deeply loves us and our world beyond measure.

I recently participated in a Bible study that centered around Genesis. I thought a lot about the relationship between God and Adam and Eve. I was struck with one thought I could not get out of my head. The very first humans to inhabit God's creation appeared to be indifferent to everything around them.

Today we might call it a sense of entitlement. The sun, the moon, the stars, the waters, and the rich kaleidoscope of life was everywhere they looked. But it was all simply there and the most beautiful place on earth was just a routine part of their daily lives.

Adam and Eve could walk and talk with God – live and in person. They could ask Him questions and get answers directly from their Creator.

God gave them so much. He gave the gift of His creation and He gave them Himself. Yet, they found themselves dissatisfied. They wanted more. Despite the vast abundance all around them, they could not help wanting something they did not have.

They were willing to risk their perfect existence. Their disobedience was grounded on a desire for that one next thing. No doubt they said to themselves, "When I have this one next thing, then I will be completely happy."

They disobeyed God by eating the fruit of the Tree of the Knowledge of Good and Evil. Then they sought to cover it up. They thought God might not notice that they had broken the rules. At the same time, they scurried around to cover up their bodies because of their new found sense of shame.

God knew what they had done before He asked. And in response to His questions, they each blamed someone else for their actions. The man blamed the woman. The woman blamed the serpent.

Who do they sound like? Can we relate to this basic fact pattern?

We have this beautiful world all around us. We have everything any rational human being could want. Yet we take it all for granted. We want more. We think that the "one next thing" will be the thing that makes us happy at last. We want it so bad that we are willing to do things we know we shouldn't.

We suffer from greed, anger and delusion as a result. We hope God will not notice or care about our transgressions. We rationalize our sins. And when we hear that still small voice asking us why we missed the mark, our first thought is to blame someone else.

The plain truth is that you and I are no better and no worse than Adam and Eve. We are flawed humans just as they were. We are sinners, just as they were. But there is one major difference. We live in the age of grace through the sacrifice of Jesus Christ.

Because of His sacrifice, I have faith that I have a spot in God's heaven. I have faith that I will have the opportunity to walk and talk with God for eternity. I don't have to worry about the father of lies. Jesus's death on the cross bought the gift of grace for us all. You are entitled to that grace as much as anyone else on earth. You may ask, "What do I have to do to claim this grace?" It is simple. Have faith in Jesus Christ the Son of God. Have faith that He was born, died and rose on the third day for all of us, that our sins may be forgiven.

My prayer for you today is to live in hope. There is hope and we can claim it and receive it through our faith in Jesus. May hope and peace be with you as you close your eyes tonight and may hope and faith awaken you in the morning to the beauty of God's new day. May you forgive yourself because you have been forgiven. May you find peace in the promise that Jesus came to earth and died on the cross to save all of us who believe in His grace.

42.

AFTERWORD

Several years ago, I began a new journey in my life, a journey that placed me on a path of complete dependence on the Lord to fulfill a commitment that I made to Him. That commitment required my trust, obedience, and direction from Him at a level that I did not know existed inside me.

We live in a world of confusion. What was once black is now white, and what was once up is now down. Is that new to this society? I don't know. Perhaps every time period was just as challenging.

One thing is true of this society we live in today: We desperately need hope. We need to know that this crazy life we are living is not all that there is. It is not the reason we were created, and it is surely not without design. We were not created to live in a haphazard world filled with ever-changing morals that shift with each new and different circumstance.

Our God is a God of order. He created and placed the sun, moon, stars, and planets in a special order, and created the ebb and flow of the tides and the cycle of the seasons. He has an order for our lives as well. We were created by a loving God. We were created with a plan and a purpose by a God who is the same today as He was yesterday and will be tomorrow. His love is so great that He suffered and died for our eternal salvation.

He has created every person that has ever been and will ever be. He has created us to be as unique as each individual snowflake and fingerprint. He has created each of us to fulfill a purpose within the uniquely individual plan that He has for us. All of these individual plans will work together for the fulfillment of God's master plan for man and for our world.

The knowledge that we were designed with an exact purpose by a loving God should give us hope. This hope can all too often get lost in our busy day to day life, in a complicated and complex society.

The essays in this book are taken from a blog that I wrote every week. For a year and a half I made a continual commitment to God to write, often with no idea as to what my subject matter would be from one week to the next. I trusted that He would give me the material and the message. He absolutely and faithfully did. I had two reasons for writing both the blog and the book you are now reading. First, I wanted to offer people hope. I wanted to share my hope in the life, death, and resurrection of Christ.

I also wanted people to think about their lives and how they were living. Were they living or merely existing? Were they living their lives under the secure umbrella of Christ or were they facing the storms in life alone and bending to the point of breaking with each bluster of wind that blows by them? The story of what our Lord has said and the way he lived and died as a human on earth should give us great freedom to live a fruitful life in a world full of beauty and purpose.

Today as I write these pages of explanation, it is Holy Saturday. Yesterday was Good Friday. The nature of this "Divine Appointment" is not lost on me.

Easter season is a time of reflection on our lives. It's a time of preparation and examination, a time to think. Holy Saturday is a day of hope. Good Friday has passed. The disciples,

Christ's mother and his followers had just witnessed His brutal death. They felt lost and abandoned. They were grieving and confused. They were scared and heartbroken.

They must have replayed his words over and over in their minds. He had told them that he would be killed, and on the third day, raised to life. (Matthew 16:21) Had they heard him correctly? Did they even understand what He had meant? How they must have agonized over every memory.

What was true? What had they imagined? As they remembered the events of the last few years, and especially the last few days, their hearts must have been pounding with fear.

How could this have happened? What did they miss? Were they to soon suffer the same agonizing death as their Teacher? What did the future hold for their fledgling movement? Was this the end? Or somehow the beginning of something bigger?

I can almost feel them holding their breath, waiting to see exactly what those words about His death and its aftermath had meant. What was going to happen next? They had to be desperately holding on to every hope, even in the face of what seemed to be a complete disaster.

With the dawn of the third day, joy did come in the morning. Jesus was raised from the dead by His Father in heaven, just as He had said. Their hope was not in vain.

Neither is ours. God's word is as strong, truthful, faithful and relevant today as it was in the days of the patriarchs. The Old Testament was fulfilled with Christ's birth, death and resurrection. His empty tomb came with the promise that all who believe in Him shall have eternal life (John 3:16).

We are now in the Lent of our lives. We live in the promise and the hope of Holy Saturday. Upon our death, as believers, we will be raised to heaven to live our eternal lives with Jesus and the Father.

That's as hopeful as it gets! We have a "Divine Appointment" with God in heaven when we pass from this world, the most incredible appointment ever made. I'll see you there!

April 2019
Travelers Rest, South Carolina

ABOUT THE AUTHOR

Cynthia Nault Smith is a native of Green Bay, Wisconsin. She moved to coastal South Carolina in her twenties and met and married her husband Dennis. They have been married for over 34 years. They have two grown sons. She lives with her husband and their Shih Tzu Maggie in the foothills of the Blue Ridge Mountains in Upstate South Carolina.

She has led many Bible Study groups and headed women's ministries at her church. She has also been on multiple mission trips to India to help spread the Gospel. This is her first book.
She is currently at work on her second book, based on the Book of Matthew.

You can reach the author with comments, thoughts, and suggestions at cjs4697@gmail.com.

57454453R00087

Made in the USA
Columbia, SC
09 May 2019